Implementing Continuous Improvement Management (CIM) in the Public Schools

Implementing Continuous Improvement Management (CIM) in the Public Schools

by

Bill Borgers

Tommy A. Thompson

SCHOLASTIC

LEADERSHIP
POLICY
RESEARCH ™

New York • Toronto • London • Auckland • Sydney

ISBN 0–590-49502–X

12 11 10 9 8 7 6 5 4 3 2 1   1 2 3 4 5/9

Printed in the U.S.A.

Library of Congress Cataloging-in-Publication Data
Borgers, Bill.
    Implementing continuous improvement management (CIM) in the public
schools/by Bill Borgers, Tommy A. Thompson.
        p. cm.
    Includes bibliographical references (p.) and index.
    ISBN 0–590–49502–X : $29.95
    1. School management and organization—Texas—Case studies. 2. Total quality
management—Texas—Case studies. I. Thompson, Tommy A. II. Title.
LB2805.B66   1994
371.2'009764—dc20   93–31779
                                                              CIP

Designed by Joan Gazdik Gillner

C O N T E N T S

It takes commitment from top management to implement CIM across an entire school district. The Dickinson district is blessed with a school board dedicated to quality teaching and learning. The district is also fortunate to have superior administrators willing to risk trying something different when such is not fashionable to do so. Continuous improvement of quality is possible only when a staff is willing to take a chance on the unknown. Dickinson's educators accepted the first step toward change by determining that all educational processes can be improved when they have the commitment to change. They have gone beyond the call of duty to serve on teams, to plan, and to train, in order to become a quality, customer-driven school district.

Our appreciation goes to Institute for Reality Therapy consultant Barbara Garner, for her work with the school district in the areas of control theory and reality therapy. Barbara is a teacher of teachers, and a close friend of both authors. Our thanks also to another friend, Dr. William Glasser, who has done so much for schools willing to follow his concepts. On several occasions he has given the district and staff his free time in order to expand our knowledge of the concepts of a quality school. Too, without the help of quality facilitators Phil Winget of Monsanto Chemical Co., and Paul Bailey of Sterling Chemical Co., CIM may have been only a dream. They have contributed their own time to train the study group in industrial uses of CIM. Our thanks also for the expertise provided by Dr. Marvin Fairman who has improved the organizational health of the district. By sharing with us information about site-based decision-making before our movement to CIM, he gave the district the head start it needed to empower workers. We must also note that productivity consultant Connie Maxfield, who helped to develop the training modules and each summer teaches Dickinson faculty how to become facilitators. She has continued, with very little reimbursement, to take an interest in the district as a consultant. Last, but certainly not least, we owe our spouses, Pat Borgers and Terry Thompson, a debt of gratitude for their patience and understanding as we labored during many nights and weekends to complete this project.

Bill Borgers, Ph.D.
Tommy A. Thompson
Dickinson, Texas
July 13, 1993

In 1990 the Dickinson Independent School District began to implement Continuous Improvement Management (CIM), using the teachings of Edwards Deming, William Glasser, and J. M. Juran to formulate a long-term plan for quality improvement. While school districts cannot expect immediate returns on their investment in CIM, Dickinson has seen a savings in operational costs through improvement of processes, a change in the morale of the district, and a willingness on the part of employees both to learn new ways and to use a team approach to solving problems. Students have experienced the difference and are responding by doing higher-quality work. Since CIM implies a complete rethinking of how to manage schools, significant improvement in student achievement is not expected until the Dickinson district has been completely transformed. CIM is not a quick-fix program.

The 6,000-student school district is located in a suburban community between Houston and Galveston, Texas. The district's students are ethnically and racially diverse, with 13 percent African American, 19 percent Hispanic, 3 percent Asian, and 65 percent Anglo–American. About 40 percent of students qualify for free or reduced meals under the federal lunch program. The Dickinson ISD is considered an average-wealth district by Texas standards.

This volume is written for campuses or districts that are considering Continuous Improvement Management. The book focuses on implementation in one school setting; however, the principles can be variously applied to a whole school district, a department, or a single classroom. It charts the transformation of a fictitious school principal and classroom teacher in their search for quality. Implementation is described sequentially, with a section of each chapter devoted to illustrating how Dickinson employees implemented the concept under discussion. In Chapters 3 through 10 the authors present information about a particular aspect of CIM that is similar to what one would learn by attending a presentation or seminar. This is followed by the adventures of a high school faculty and principal in transforming knowledge into reality. The presentation gives the reader the concepts of CIM, and the characters bring home the real-life application.

A system-feedback section summarizes the ideas presented, and this is followed by an examination of the Dickinson experience in implementing the concepts introduced in the chapter. Each chapter ends with a summary of management principles used.

A Tale of Two Wagon Trains

Centuries from now, a historian of American public education reform should have no problem tracing a well-marked trail of change, starting with publication of *A Nation at Risk* in 1983. He or she would however earn a head of gray hair in reading blizzards of research, published in the 1980s, cataloguing the failures of the late twentieth century American public school, and would begin collecting on a retirement pension before completing an analysis of the thousands of experiments at reform in the nation's approximately 100,000 schools during that decade.

The historian likely would shake his or her head, however, at the lack of measurable progress in both student achievement and school-system management efficiency as a result of this waterfall of change. Indeed, it may in the future appear as one of the modern wonders of the world that such an expenditure of resources as the reform efforts of the 1980s produced so little in quantifiable results.

A growing number of educators, policymakers, and parents are coming to believe that the lack of clear student-achievement gains proves that the very term reform has been a misnomer for the changes of the past ten years. To reform means to form again—to make into a new form or essence. Few of the reforms since *A Nation at Risk* have truly changed the form of public education. At best, reform has concentrated efforts and resources on getting more of the same type of product out of the old form, which is a "factory" model of schooling that has remained essentially the same since the United States emerged as an industrial power over 100 years ago.

While the system of public schooling reflects so little transformation, American society as a whole, and most acutely the work force, has experienced a sea change. Today's employees are expected to work collaboratively to create the synergy that post–Industrial Age competitiveness deems of more value than individual effort, yet today's schools for the most part operate on a competitive grading system that prepares students for an academic career based on individual effort. Today's employees are expected to learn specifics as such become relevant, applying them with the aid of critical thinking and analysis. In most modern American schools, however, the inculcation of facts and specifics is emphasized over the fostering of reasoning abilities, as if to imply that the work force will require a daily recitation of the Laws of Thermodynamics or the Amendments to the Constitution.

In short, most of today's schools prepare youngsters for tasks they are—and probably will remain—seldom required to perform, loading their heads with information they will rarely find occasion to use. And, despite the earnest attempts of educators to bring technology into the classroom, in order both to give teachers more freedom to try new techniques and to meet the nonacademic needs of students in our increasingly fragmented society, education in 1994 plods on for the most part as uninspired and out of touch with real-world demands as it was in 1984.

It is hoped that it will not be in anecdotes that a diligent historian will see, a century from now, the first glimmerings in the 1990s of a truly fundamental change in the public education system that, for perhaps the first time in more than 100 years, aligned the needs of society with the product that is the process of education. That system is known by several terms: Continuous Improvement Management (CIM), Total Quality Management (TQM), Deming management, Quality schools, and Glasser Schools. These approaches are truly reforms because they do involve a new form for education, one created outside of the century-old paradigm, or model, of public schools.

If there is a central tenet in this new form for education, it would have to be "Know thy customer." Indeed, the process of education in a Continuous Improvement (CIM) system is linked by two-way communication to the ever-changing needs of all the customers of education—students, educators themselves, employers, the government, and taxpayers.

Most of the concepts of CIM are simple, even deceptively so. To know the needs of one's customers appears to be an easy task, and certainly a goal with which few people would quibble. But to restructure what is taught, how it is taught, and even who teaches it, in order to meet the needs of the customers—now, that's an entirely different story. And it's a story that this book is all about.

To grasp CIM in a public school setting, the reader must continue to ask, "Am I thinking about education in the old or the new form?" There should be little similarity between the ways in which a fully integrated CI school and the traditional American "factory model" school operate. To aid your focus on the new mind-set of CI schools, perhaps a revisionist view of American frontier history will shed a little light. But be sure to put your newest thinking cap on before you read the following tale of two wagon trains, one led by Boss A. Lot and the other led by Lead M. On.

A TALE OF TWO WAGON TRAINS

Hundreds of thousands of adventurous Americans settled the West in the mid-to-late 1800s by traveling to the land of opportunity in trains of covered wagons. Eastern newspapers daily bannered the dangers of the westward journeys, and relatives and neighbors cautioned against leaving the comforts of home and hearth for a brave new world.

The perceived perils and well-meaning advice didn't deter the new arrivals to the West, although those who chose to make the journey differed in the strength of their convictions and courage. Over a period of time, it could be detected that there were three groups of people who joined the wagon trains—explorers, scouts, and settlers.

The *explorers* were a small but hearty band, known for taking risks and making the most of their limited knowledge of the unknown. They were willing to map the new land through (often disastrous) trial and error, charging over passes, fording rushing waters, and traversing parched and lifeless plains.

Using the explorers' maps, a group of *scouts* would appear, fleshing out details and specifics for others to follow. Scouts had the limited comfort of learning the explorers' mistakes, but nonetheless encountered a hefty share of harrowing moments in the wilderness. Back East, the city dwellers eagerly awaited news from the frontier. They learned at first the sensational tales of adventure and intrigue from the explorers, then heard the solid stories of progress from the scouts.

At first a trickle, then a mighty flow, the *settlers* hitched their futures to a westward star and moved to the Big Country along paths already rutted by the wheels of both the explorers and scouts. They quickly became the majority group, establishing the patterns of life that in their minds civilized the West.

Of course, back East there were always the naysayers, that minority but vocal group of melancholy souls who bemoaned the loss of the old ways. They saw the westward expansion in terms of its impact on their community, and adjudged it a threat. The latest dispatch bearing news of difficulty out West enlivened their spirits, filling them with a momentary rush of hope that the frontier experiment would finally collapse and their former neighbors would return home.

Boss A. Lot seldom had problems selling seats on his wagons, at least in the early days after the scouts had blazed the trails. His reputation was as a leader who was firmly in charge and never in doubt. You could always expect a quick answer from Boss, and he never wavered in making a decision. He of course surrounded himself with wagoneers and crew members who held the same strong characteristics.

Boss set specific goals for his wagoneers for each day of the trip west, never yielding even on days with adverse circumstances common to travel in those days, such as flash floods, rattlesnake-bitten horses, and snapped wagon poles. Boss exhorted his wagoneers to reach their goals at all costs, and his crew responded with cutthroat competitiveness that verged on all-out war. In fact, his wagoneers routinely were called before him to answer charges that they had hired operatives to sabotage competing wagons. Boss professed great outrage at the dirty tricks, but was overheard remarking to his assistant: "That's the name of the game in this dog-eat-dog world." He seemed to believe that competitiveness sharpened the skills of his subordinates.

If a wagoneer failed to meet Boss's standards, he could expect swift retribution—usually a demotion to the rear of the train. What developed was a pecking order of wagon trains, with the wagoneer who had outlasted the others in front, and the latest "screwup" in the dust. Boss also gave the front wagons extra supplies and equipment, sometimes taking from the end of the trail to give to the leader. Of course, no one questioned him on this practice. If they had, he would have responded by saying it was his decision, and he ran the show. Like the crew members said, everyone knew where Boss stood.

Over time, Boss perfected his system for meeting quotas. He hired wagon-train monitors to time the wagons for a three-hour period each day. Wagoneers were ranked each week by average distance covered. To motivate the wagoneers, Boss labeled below-average wagons with gray-colored canvas banners that read "Slow Wagon." Wagons that remained above the average received monthly bonuses. Boss believed that this competition kept the wagon trains at peak performance.

Passengers on Boss's wagons learned to greet the head man with a mixture of fear and obedience, addressing him only when talked to first. They were told upon embarking that children were to be seen and not heard, so the passengers spent a considerable amount of time quieting their young ones. Boss made it clear that passengers were in the hands of capable wagoneers who could lead them through unforeseen perils only with complete cooperation. No thinking was needed from the passengers, just obedience, Boss said. He dealt with problems by posting new rules in front of each wagon as needed. This system provided for clear communication between the passengers and wagoneers.

Because of the considerable and often unforeseen delays involved in overland wagon travel, Boss knew that management of the food and water supplies was key to a successful journey. During passages through the Rockies, it was a matter of life or death if the wagoneers had not made sufficient provision. Boss devised an elaborate food-and-water ration system based on actual consumption: As unexpected delays occurred, he asked his wagoneers to reduce their rations by 10 percent, and used his monitors to determine the true consumption of provisions. Wagons that did not reduce consumption by 10 percent were posted for everyone to see, and 20 percent of that month's salary was withheld from the offending wagoneer.

Passengers often complained that it was not fair to penalize an entire wagon, nor was it just to compare consumption among wagons. Boss dismissed such complaints as examples of lazy passengers who refused to cooperate for the good of the whole. Once, a group of passengers attempted to show Boss evidence that their wagoneer was withholding food and water supplies from them in order to meet a reduction quota. The wagoneer had received a 20 percent bonus from Boss for his outstanding management efforts, but the passengers had caught on to the game—or so they said. Boss waved the complaints away as further examples of jealous passengers who were on the "losing end" of the train.

Boss's management career itself was cut short after a couple of years. The Department of the Interior shut down his operation after conducting a Blue Ribbon Committee hearing on complaints from his customers, many of whom said the fighting among the wagoneers was more perilous than the trip's natural hazards. Others presented evidence that Boss's daily travel quotas put undue pressure on the wagons, causing equipment failure and consequent delays that seemed to grow worse with each trip.

Actually, things pretty well took care of themselves. In October 1853, Boss led his last trip out West. The next spring, a scout found the deteriorated remains of his wagons in a dead-end canyon a quarter of the way up a mountain pass. The passengers had abandoned the wagons and scattered for outposts. Boss's body was found under a pile of sagebrush and wagon-train policy books, in an apparent last-ditch effort to keep from freezing to death.

Curiously, the scouts found stashes of food in some wagons but no food in others. Boss's journal did not include any reference to impending danger, although those of the wagoneers and passengers fairly screamed out with concerns. Wagons had been breaking down daily, strife among the competing wagons was at fever pitch, and so on, yet Boss apparently had heard of none of the problems.

The Federal Bureau of Wagon Train Safety's report on the disaster concluded the following:

1. Lack of communication and fear caused those who knew about impending dangers to keep the information to themselves.

2. Excessive costs tied to the regulation and monitoring of the operation (monitors, policy books) diverted resources that could have been used to keep equipment in good working order.

3. Dust kicked up by the front wagons caused damage to the wagons in the rear, increasing repair costs and slowing down the entire train. It appears that this problem was never looked at by Boss, nor was it mentioned by the wagoneers in the front of the train.

4. The distribution system for food and water was inequitable, favoring some for allegedly meeting quotas and penalizing others for supposedly not meeting them. (The passengers rarely were told about the quotas, but suffered the consequences nonetheless.)

5. Boss disregarded the scouts' maps, and consequently had little direction in his mission.

Lead M. On, one of the surviving wagon masters, studied the pitfalls of his former boss's ill-fated ventures for most of the next year. He visited with as many explorers and scouts as he could identify, then persuaded a small group to join with him in developing a successful wagon train so that westward expansion could resume. Early the next year, the group identified its mission, which was to reach the West before winter with all wagon-train passengers in good health. Cost of the trip would remain constant, or be reduced, to ensure affordable passage for all who wanted to settle in the new land of opportunity. Lead's goal was to create such a pleasurable wagon-train experience that passengers would write home, bragging about their new life and the easy passage to it. Lead knew that a quality wagon train would spin off many more benefits, resulting in a win—win situation for all involved.

Reflecting on Boss's ill-fated ventures, the new group realized they had to do more than just do things right. They also had to do the right things. If a quality system for conveying settlers to their new land could be created from the onset, the Lead Wagon Train Co. could keep costs low and thus attract a significant market share. So the experienced group set to work on a quality plan, long before a single wagon rutted a dusty trail.

Lead and his inner circle of explorers and scouts came to consensus on a management system for wagon trains, then developed a plan to train everyone in this new management style. Lead then contacted the initial passengers who had purchased tickets for the journey. These anxious adventurers were asked to develop the details of a plan that would support the mission, that of a timely and healthy journey. Much to their initial surprise, the passengers soon became ardently involved in the task of deciding how the wagon trains would be organized, the type and amount of supplies needed for the trip, and the roles of each person in the wagon train. The explorers, scouts, and passengers met each day to compare information, share ideas and finalize the plan.

To direct the course of the wagon train, a steering team was organized from members of each wagon. Lead gave each team the authority and responsibility to investigate the challenges facing the travelers, and to make the needed changes when a consensus was formed.

Lead made two other important decisions before the first trip. First, he didn't purchase his wagons by the low-bid process, as Boss had done. Rather, he developed a working relationship with a major wagon manufacturer, Quality First Wagon Co. He collected data indicating that Quality First's wagons experienced 20 percent fewer breakdowns per 1,000 miles than the industry average. That, in Lead's mind, justified the higher cost of Quality First's wagons.

Second, Lead asked his scouts and explorers to develop ongoing training for the passengers in all aspects of wagon-train operation. Each person on the trip would learn to spot defects and opportunities on a daily basis, and also would learn appropriate problem-solving skills sufficient to take care of difficulties as they arose. Wagoneers thus developed their own system for collecting data on the performance of their wagons, and assessing potential signs of breakdown.

Comfortable with the initial training and planning he and his group had invested in the new venture, Lead approached the first journey with cautious optimism. Instinctively, he believed the tremendous amount of time spent in training everyone would pay off, despite the derisive comments he heard on the streets, where naysayers were making comparisons between Lead's wagons and Noah's ark. Lead did have moments of doubt, though, and so decided in the last hours to bring along extra personnel—wagon mechanics and monitors—and a couple of additional wagons. Better to be safe than sorry, he figured.

As the wagons plodded across the plains, Lead felt a deep satisfaction with the way the new system was operating. Wagoneers enthusiastically kept records and collected data on the performance of the wagons. Of particular interest were the types and frequencies of noises that occurred on the wagons. After extensive data collection, the wagoneers discovered that certain noises were most frequent before breakdowns. The wagoneers developed a preventive-maintenance system in response to the new information, greatly reducing breakdowns. This reduction created only one challenge: What to do with the mechanics whose services were not needed?

Lead's group knew that the wagon train had to cover a certain average number of miles each day to get over the mountain pass before winter. A realistic person, he knew there would be days, such as those experienced by Boss's wagon trains, where everything went wrong. Lead wouldn't respond with more dictates and exhortations, however. Instead, he calculated the average number of miles the train needed to travel per day to reach destination before winter. He then determined an upper standard and lower standard of miles to travel each day. As long as the wagon train's mileage remained within those limits, Lead saw no need to change the operations of the outfit.

If the train experienced a week of below-standard mileage, Lead didn't respond with pressure on wagoneers. Rather, he assigned a team to study possible reasons for the slowdown, and offer a plan to increase mileage. Lead even assigned a team to discover why the wagon train had exceeded its upper standard of mileage on certain weeks. By analyzing the performance of the wagon train, the entire organization benefited by learning how to improve performance through data-based information.

Over a period of years, Lead's charts on wagon-train performance, displayed in hallways in the new company office, indicated a curious phenomenon. As teams of explorers, scouts, and settlers analyzed wagon-train data and made reasoned changes in operations, the average mileage covered per week increased. Within three years, Lead's company reduced its ticket price because of improved efficiency, and increased market share. He also formed a partnership with the Quality First Wagon Co. in order to improve the manufacture and maintenance of the wagons. Lead's wagoneers shared performance information with Quality First, while Quality First trained the wagoneers in advanced wagon repair.

Recalling the bitterness and squabbles that broke out because of Boss's food-and-water allocation system, Lead and his team of explorers and scouts created a plan that allowed each settler to chart personal consumption each week. Passengers kept their own records and calculated their wagon's average weekly consumption, then developed the upper and lower standard. Wagon teams analyzed the data, to help make changes that stabilized the week-to-week food consumption and even allowed the train to implement waste-reduction measures. The wagon-train council, composed of representatives from all the wagons, decided that food saved by the waste-reduction efforts was to be shared with all wagons in the train.

Within five years, Lead's wagon-train company further reduced ticket prices and increased its market share. Wagon-train industry analysts on Wall Street reported that westward migration had increased 33 percent within this brief time span primarily because of the breakthrough in wagon transportation developed by Lead and his team.

Despite all the success, however, Lead's company continued to face three thorny problems related to the environment: conflict with Indians, fires, and fording mountain streams. In dealing with the Indians, a team of passengers met with Indian chiefs to work out a plan that would meet the needs of both sides, thus avoiding conflict and violence. From that point on, extra provisions were stocked for use in bargaining with the Indians.

Firefighting was a constant problem because of poor campfire management techniques, a problem inherited from the old style of Boss's days. Lead's steering team analyzed the practice of fire management, and developed a better way. Soon, Lead found he was spending almost no time fighting fires.

Another team developed a better way to cross streams by building bridges upstream rather than downstream. No one had ever done it that way, but it seemed only logical to cross streams at their narrowest point. Flush with progress, the team went on to develop a system for temporarily damming streams for wagon-train crossings. The tests proved successful, and from that time on, Lead always went upstream to solve problems.

Twenty years later, reflecting on a career that literally opened the floodgates of opportunity for new settlers, Lead felt a deep sense of satisfaction—not at his own accomplishments, but at those of literally thousands of people. It had been years since settlers had hesitated to make the trip west because of the poor quality of the wagon trains. Unlike the competition, Lead's wagons posed little risk for the passengers. In place of competition, he had developed partnerships based on mutual respect with the environment, suppliers, and the Indians. A cooperative spirit existed at all levels of his organization, and was duly felt by the customers. There were clearly understood collaborative processes for solving problems. Wagoneers spent only minutes each day fighting fires along the road. And so on.

Doing it the right way from the beginning wasn't such a gambler's risk after all, Lead concluded. His people solved their own problems—without blame, punishment, or fear. And the entire nation was the better for it.

CHAPTER 2

Getting Started

THE PRINCIPAL

Trail's End Middle School principal Pat Ann Hold administers a typical American middle school, one that its community would probably rate a B for effectiveness. Astute observers of the local educational system would say, however, that no greater than 20 percent of Trail's End's students perform at a world-class quality level.

Despite twenty years in education, and the popular support of parents and her community, Pat knew that Trail's End was a long way from where it could be. In quiet moments at home, she pondered whether the school was in fact failing its community. After all, almost four in ten students dropped out before graduating from high school, failure rates approached 50 percent in some classes, and discipline referrals were on a steady incline.

Pat faced her underlying doubts with an energetic personality and a willingness to change, but she had to admit to herself that she had no idea what or how to change. The school was doing everything that any other 1990s middle school would do to provide a sound instructional program. Moreover, there were few moments during the work day to think about a new direction. Breaking up fights, requisitioning new desks, and presiding over after-school committee meetings drained the natural energy from her well before she left the campus around 6 P.M. It was in the waning minutes of a particularly stressful Monday that a long-time friend who worked for a nearby manufacturing company called and invited her to a workshop on CIM in the next week.

Pat came home from the presentation convinced that her school was managed more like Boss's wagon train than Lead's. The last six years had seen six new programs introduced as quick fixes to problems associated with student achievement and discipline. Two of the programs were mandated from the central office, and the other four were the outcome of ideas she gleaned from workshops or from visiting other schools. Not one program had achieved its goal, Pat thought—although she had to admit that she had no evaluation process in place in any of the programs. Along with most of her peers at Trail's End, a new program was judged a success if it "seemed like it works" or if "students seem to like it." She and her campus stood on unsettled ground as change swelled in waves around her. Faced daily with this sinking feeling, which spread like a virus throughout the staff as the year progressed, Pat agonized about how she could introduce this exciting new approach called CIM to her school.

After several days observing the characteristics of her diverse staff, Pat came to the conclusion that paralleled the observation about the three different types of westward settlers. She decided to follow Lead's example and begin meeting with the explorers, settlers, and scouts in the school. She counted several teachers—henceforth the explorers—on her staff who were always trying new ideas. On a calm gray winter afternoon, a day reflective of the diminished hopes and fast-fading spirits of teachers not quite halfway through the year, Pat met with explorer teachers representing all departments, to hash out the potential impact of Continuous Improvement Management on the school. Working from her notes on the CIM presentation, the group first brainstormed ideas about how a quality school would "look." From the description, they developed a mission statement that succinctly stated where they wanted to be in five, ten, and twenty years. The focus was on quality student work.

Once a mission statement was in place, Pat began to realize the enormity of the mind-set change that her staff would be asked to make. If she had learned one concept early in the CIM experience, it was that people change when they see the necessity of moving past the status quo. Otherwise, the inertia of the way things are will never be overcome by the possibilities of the way things can be. The only realistic approach to fostering the imperative shift in thinking is to focus the staff on training, she concluded. That in itself was a break from tradition in her district, where staff development was an underfunded and unfocused activity that had as its purpose to offer only the bare minimum that the state said teachers required. Initially, Pat knew that more training was needed for her and the group of risk-takers. She sat at her desk and composed a memo to all members of the risk-taker group, and anyone else interested, inviting what she hoped would be an enlarging circle of the staff to attend the next presentation.

Pat was anxious to know what she could do with regard to the teachers in order to get them to adopt this new philosophy.

THE TEACHER

Will E. Survive was a risk-taker who eagerly tried new strategies to reach his students. He attended most training sessions the school offered, in search of new answers. Regardless of what he tried, however, it appeared that only 20 percent of his students cared about grades. Most of the remaining students were not mentally participating in class. Homework assignments were rarely turned in on time.

Each year, Will gritted his teeth at the end of every grading period as he curved test scores to keep the failure rate from topping the 20 percent level he had learned in college was the maximum any teacher should fail. Because he maintained a good rapport with students, there seldom was a need for discipline in his class. Indeed, his classroom seemed an oasis of calm in a sea of choppy waters, because as a whole Trail's End was experiencing increasing student discipline problems.

Will was one of the most involved teachers in the school, serving simultaneously on school committees to improve discipline, better lunchroom behavior, and decrease vandalism. He was disgruntled that the tone of most of the meetings was negative; blaming students for the problems was typically followed by enacting more rules to control them. Will knew that the committees were dealing with symptoms rather than problems, but he didn't know a better direction. Besides, the committee recommendations were vetoed by the principal more than half of the time. There always was a reason something couldn't be done.

Nevertheless, Will continued to forge ahead, despite pangs of doubt about his effectiveness with students. Standing in his doorway after the end of classes and watching the passing adolescent parade, he often thought jokingly to himself that being an airline controller would be less stressful than dealing with the impossible demands he faced each school day.

When Pat asked Will to be part of a group to examine a new concept called Continuous Improvement Management, he enthusiastically agreed to participate. Will was acutely aware that he was staring burnout in the face and losing the battle. This new information maybe—just maybe—would spark another cycle of enthusiasm. He hoped it was not just one more easy-come, easy-go program. He was tired of doing things to students in attempts to motivate them.

THE DICKINSON EXPERIENCE

Getting started with CIM does not require an extensive knowledge of its principles. For example, the Dickinson Independent School District began its journey into CIM with the assistance of two chemical refinery quality trainers who lived in the community. The key is to capture the attention of interested persons, moving increasingly toward involving a critical mass of the leaders and risk-takers in the school. Planning how to introduce CIM requires committed people.

In Dickinson all administrators studied the principles of CIM for nine months before developing a strategy for districtwide implementation. Top-down commitment is vital to achieve bottom-up empowerment. Whether at a district central office or at a school, a study group of eight to fifteen people is ideal. It doesn't hurt to seek the input of a few "cracker-barrel" leaders as an addition to the study group. Cracker-barrel leaders are persons who, like the conversationalists of bygone days around the wood stove at the local general store, are valued for their opinions. All organizations have some cracker-barrel leaders whose opinions are trusted by a segment of the membership. Including parents can be beneficial, especially when the parents work at one of the rapidly growing number of companies that are using CIM principles.

CIM requires breaking the mold of conventional thinking. A study group will be creating a new system, not just tinkering with the old system. A decade of reform has demonstrated that the Information Age requires schools that will effectively educate all students, not just the top 20 percent of learners who always have been served well by the schools. No matter how much leaders tinker with the present system, it is not capable of serving the majority of today's students with quality. It is time to recreate the system. CIM is a proven way to shape and to manage this new system.

The product of the study group is a plan for introducing CIM to the rest of the staff and community. The plan should contain the organizational structure needed to maintain focus, the membership of the initial committees, and the plan for providing training. Care must be taken to communicate often with the faculty regarding the progress of the initial group. The study group should eventually be open to anyone wanting to join. Leadership must guard against the study group's being perceived as a secretive, elite body that is up to no good.

MANAGEMENT PRINCIPLES USED

An outline of the management principles used in implementing particular aspects of CIM will conclude chapters 2–10. Managing involves four primary activities: organizing, planning, controlling, and leading. Implementing CIM requires a change from the status quo in all four aspects of management. The change to CIM requires *organizing* a new structure for school-district operations. This structural change will place heightened emphasis on *planning* to achieve results. Management will as never before be required to engage in *controlling* in order to ensure the organization's capability to perform the required tasks. And finally, CIM will not work unless a new style of *leading*, characterized by collaborative rather than unilateral decision-making, takes place.

ORGANIZING

1. Identify risk-takers in the faculty.
2. Ask risk-takers to volunteer for a study group that will meet periodically during the year.
3. Set a regularly scheduled time, place, and date for meetings.
4. Gather CIM resources to use for study.
5. Develop an agenda for each meeting.
6. Allow time for intensive discussion of issues and new learning.

PLANNING

1. After one school year of study, lead the group toward developing a plan for introducing CIM to the faculty.
2. The plan should include the organizational structure for decision-making and communication.
3. What future role will the study-group members play?
4. What functions need to be assigned to the committee(s) overseeing the stages of implementation?

CONTROLLING

Use a discrepancy continuum to get direction from the study group.

EXAMPLE

1. Place an X on the continuum that best represents your group's assessment of the principle under study.

Principle: All tests should be open-book.

Current Practice

```
0   1   2   3   4   5   6   7   8   9   10
not a practice                      very prevalent
```

Desired

```
0   1   2   3   4   5   6   7   8   9   10
not a practice                      very prevalent
```

Discrepancy between current and desired _____

2. Subtract the current practice value from the desired value to determine discrepancy.

3. Use high-discrepancy values to form the school's Quality School Correlates (see Chapter 8).

4. Be sure to receive consensus from the study group for the commitment to the new philosophy.

LEADING

1. Use a consultant, or have the principal facilitate the study group.
2. The principal and other school leaders must be involved in the group.

Enlightenment

M odern management theory places specific names on the diametrically opposed styles of leadership seen in the two wagon trains led by Boss and Lead respectively. Dictatorial management that emphasizes achievement of arbitrary, specific production goals is commonly called management by results, or boss management. Management by consensus, with an emphasis on continuous, incremental improvement, is commonly termed lead management. To delineate between the two methods, it is important to learn the definition of a system, and how it pertains to management. A system is merely a method for explaining the activities of organizations. A simple system is depicted below:

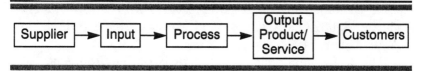

ENVIRONMENT

Each employee in an organization owns at least one process: an operation, task, or series of activities performed as part of the routine of work. Most employees own or use several processes during a day of work. Teachers primarily use two processes: instructing, and managing. Instructing is easy if the students want to be instructed. If they do not, which is the dilemma facing the vast majority of teachers, the teacher must become a manager in order to produce quality.

Managing is a process used to get people to do something when they are not motivated to do it. Most classroom teachers spend 80 percent of their time managing and 20 percent instructing. It is no surprise, then, that teaching is a stressful job. Teachers would agree that the goal is to do more instructing and less managing. CIM is all about how to manage in a way that allows a person to become a facilitator and coach rather than a traditional boss.

All processes have an input and an output. An input may be a curriculum guide, textbook, information, or supplies. An input is anything that is needed to help perform the process.

The process transforms the inputs into outputs, which therefore are the products of the process. To use a simple example, typing is a process performed primarily by clerical employees. The inputs to typing are written communications and verbal messages. The process is the mechanical striking of keys on a machine.

An output is a product or service produced by the process; the product of typing is a memorandum, paper, or manuscript. Inputs need suppliers, and outputs are produced for customers. Some suppliers are internal to the organization, and others are external. Using the school system as an example, parents, textbook publishers, and state education agencies are external suppliers. Third-grade teachers are internal suppliers to the fourth-grade teachers. When administrators provide funding and resources to teachers, they are the internal suppliers. The roles change, depending on the process.

Customers are the users of the product or service. There are both internal and external customers. External customers are parents, businesses, colleges, and armed services. Examples of internal customers are ninth-grade teachers who receive students from the eighth grade, and clerical staff who receive directions from management.

The last component of a system is the environment. The environment consists of all outside influences on the system. In a school system the decisions, attitudes, and priorities of the community, local businesses, and the state legislature are examples of environmental influences.

Understanding the components of a system will help explain those used by Boss and Lead. Boss used a detection system of management, while Lead used a prevention system.

The *detection* system uses mass inspection at the end of the process, to determine whether a product is adequate for customer use. This uniquely American management system typically produces inferior products that reveal their defects during consumption or use. If an inspection judges a product to be defective, the product is either reworked or recycled. Reworking is expensive and innately inefficient, but not as costly as defect recycling.

Detection system   **Environment**

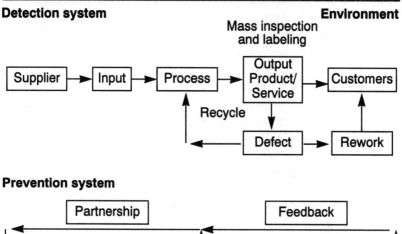

Prevention system

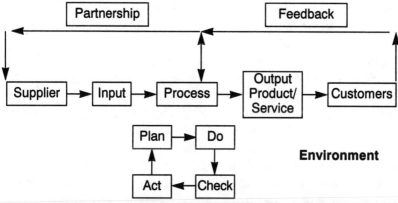

The detection process has ongoing inefficiencies that result in additional costs—for mass inspection, for recalling the product, and for losing customers because of product failure that causes dissatisfaction. The system attempts to correct the problem downstream, at the end stages of the process.

Schools have much the same system for inspection, relying as they do on mass inspection of the product (students) through grades and norm-referenced tests. Schools have rework rooms and even rework schools for defective students, and student recycling occurs with every grade retention. This is a costly system, given that it produces world-class quality in no more than 20 percent of students.

The prevention system does not utilize mass inspection downstream in the process. Sampling, rather than mass inspection, is used to determine the quality of the finished product. Inspection is the task of the worker, the process owner. All workers self-assess the quality of their product. If defects are noted by the worker, then the process is improved either by the individual or through team problem-solving methods. The process is improved beginning as far upstream as possible. The further upstream a process can be improved, the less the product will need improvement downstream. The worker is empowered to use a problem-solving method called plan-do-check/study-act, which is discussed in greater detail in Chapter 7.

Management's role is to develop trust within the system, remove barriers for workers, and provide information for problem-solving. Two other components are customer feedback and supplier partnerships. The needs of the customer are valued and changeable; management must develop methods to determine these on a continuous basis. Management and workers may produce a product that meets rigorous specifications with almost zero defects, but if the product does not meet customer needs or is not produced when the customer needs it, the production has been a waste of time and resources. Therefore, continuous feedback is required to improve the design of the product in order to fit the customer's needs. Forming partnerships with the suppliers helps guarantee quality inputs, since it is difficult to produce quality products if the inputs are sadly defective. A true partnership consists of what the supplier can do for the purchaser, and vice versa. The purpose of the partnership is to receive supplies at the best possible quality and cost. This involves sharing information and technology and working together for the common good, rather than spending precious energy protecting competitive "secrets." The prevention system is more adaptable to environmental constraints because it is a system built on planning. New constraints are recognized as quality opportunities and solved by using Quality Process Control (QPC) tools, such as those described in Chapter 6.

Quality managers gain an understanding of the system so they can identify their processes, suppliers, and customers, both internal and external. After identifying each, a method for receiving feedback from the customers should be put in place. Customers' needs should be met within the capability of the process to meet them. Parents may want their childrens' school to provide one computer for each student, to improve instruction, but if it is not within the capability of the school to fund several hundred computers and train everyone on using them, the school simply cannot meet the customers' needs.

Continuous improvement means that all components of the process are to be the subject of study: The capability of the entire process should be continuously improved. Top management should make changes to the system to improve the skills, working conditions, and tools of the workers. These changes must be accomplished in a noncoercive manner without evaluations, grading, ranking or other means used to cajole workers into working harder. The main problem is how we manage, not how diligently the worker works.

For school pracitioners of CIM, the question of where students fit into system thinking must be discussed and answered. What is a student—a product, worker, client, prospective customer, customer, all of these or none? If management classifies the student as a product, then most likely the system is based on inspection and coercion. Boss treated the settlers like products rather than customers. A product can be sorted, labeled, grouped, reworked, recycled, graded, and ranked. Not one of these methods has produced world-class quality. What happens to our mind-set when the student is viewed as a customer or worker? Both designations require that the student be involved in the process of producing the product, which is learning. If more schools would change from treating students as products, to treating them as customers or fellow workers, then schools would take the first giant leap toward becoming quality learning-producing systems.

PRINCIPAL PAT ANN HOLD

Pat and her study group met again to discuss the presentation and put finishing touches on the group's plan for introducing CIM at the school. All of the study-team members brainstormed a list of processes they owned, internal and external customers and suppliers, and inputs and outputs of their system. They also brainstormed ways they could communicate with each part of the system. It was decided to set up customer/supplier meetings to discover more about customer needs, and to what degree the school could meet those needs. The goal of the customer/supplier meetings would be a partnership agreement designed to improve the quality of the product or service. Students, as customers or workers, needed to understand how to define quality in their school work and lives alike. The teachers who were out in front as explorers agreed to begin discussing quality with students. The plan for introducing quality to the rest of the staff called for a steering committee to oversee training and planning for quality. The plan called for the principal to select one-third of the members of the committee, taking into account the ethnicity of the staff and representation from all grade levels or subject areas. The faculty would select one-third by popular vote. The remaining one-third would be parents and community members selected by the study group. The facilitator for the steering committee would be the principal. The number of members on the steering committee was between 15 percent and 20 percent of the staff.

The steering committee met to adopt a mission statement for the committee. The study group's mission statement was revised, and communicated to the faculty. It was decided that all members would attend the presentations and read everything they could find and share on quality. To gain information from the teachers who were willing to jump in and begin using CIM in the classroom, the steering committee formed an advisory group. Their role would be to try to experiment with ideas pertaining to quality management, and report the results to the steering committee. The membership on the advisory committee would be extended to any faculty member agreeing with the new mission statement. Pat wanted the mission statement to rally everyone to improvement. It was read at the beginning of every meeting, and posted in every class for everyone to read. The mission statement became the driving force for the two committees. The primary focus was on quality learning by the students.

Pat felt confident that what she was doing for the staff would help sell the changes that were needed. However, Pat was still fighting fires most of the time. There was very little visible evidence that people had changed or that students were benefiting from the new approach. In fact, the surveys from the parents, businesses, and students alike indicated that things were worse than she believed. It all only seemed to uncover more problems— but at least now Pat looked at the problems with a ray of hope.

TEACHER WILL E. SURVIVE

Will was selected for the advisory committee, where he could experiment with the new philosophy. He examined all the processes he owned—instructing, managing, planning, clerical work, and others. Will concluded that his customers were the students, the parents (when delivering information on amount of learning produced), and the teachers who would subsequently teach his students. His primary suppliers were the parents (when teaching and managing), curriculum developers, textbook publishers, the principal, and previous teachers. Will wanted the outputs to be meaningful learning, self-esteem, and responsibility. He knew he would have to improve his processes and inputs in order to achieve quality outputs. He believed all students could learn what was needed to know in his subject, if only he could figure out how to do it.

The first step for Will was to get feedback from his customers, the students and parents. He surveyed students on classroom conditions and practices that best suited their styles of learning. He asked the parents what they thought their children should know after completing his class. He took time to involve the students in developing a class mission statement that reflected what and how they wanted to learn. Will had to admit he was somewhat surprised at the level of interest from his students, who contributed well-thought-out comments about the learning process that proved to him that they were not "brain dead," as a fellow faculty member had suggested. The students' mission statement was posted, and used as an evaluation for each unit taught. Next, he introduced the concept of quality. He devoted the last 10 minutes of several periods over a span of time to a quality circle discussion on the topic "What is quality?" (A quality circle is a structured, open-ended discussion of a relevant and thought-provoking topic.)

Will had used quality circles in the past to clarify topics. But now he saw a better use: He would devote time each week to a quality circle discussion, in order to get to know his students better, improve their speaking and listening skills, and receive feedback from them. The directions for the holding of a quality circle are as follows:

1. The students should be seated in a circle.
2. The facilitator's role is to ask questions and for clarification. The facilitator should neither interject regularly nor provide answers.
3. The rules are simple: Raise your hand if want to talk, don't insult others.

To structure the proceedings, the leader should develop defining, personalizing, and challenging-type questions. *Defining* questions deal with who, what, when, where, and how. *Personalizing* questions solicit opinions, judgments, and comparisons; they draw on the personal experiences of the students. *Challenge* questions ask students to analyze, create, problem-solve, or play the role of devil's advocate on an issue. It took Will several quality circle discussions to feel comfortable and for the students to begin expressing themselves. They initially were not comfortable with questions that did not have pat answers.

Will conducted this quality circle over several class periods because he wanted to proceed slowly in helping the students to define quality. Normally, a quality circle would last 10 to 15 minutes, leaving the students anxious for the next discussion. Will used the following balloon structure for developing his questions.

BALLOONS

ICEBREAKER—Finish this stem: Quality is...

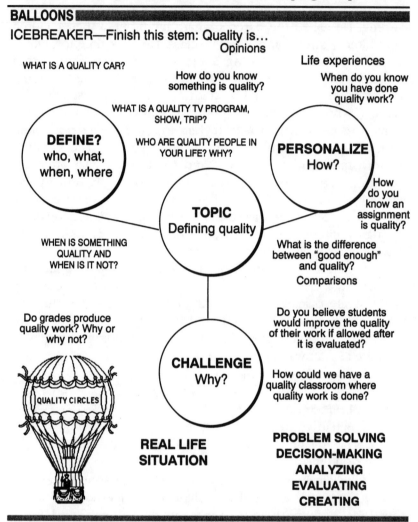

Opinions

WHAT IS A QUALITY CAR?

How do you know something is quality?

Life experiences

When do you know you have done quality work?

WHAT IS A QUALITY TV PROGRAM, SHOW, TRIP?

DEFINE?
who, what, when, where

WHO ARE QUALITY PEOPLE IN YOUR LIFE? WHY?

PERSONALIZE
How?

How do you know an assignment is quality?

TOPIC
Defining quality

WHEN IS SOMETHING QUALITY AND WHEN IS IT NOT?

What is the difference between "good enough" and quality?

Comparisons

Do grades produce quality work? Why or why not?

CHALLENGE
Why?

Do you believe students would improve the quality of their work if allowed after it is evaluated?

How could we have a quality classroom where quality work is done?

QUALITY CIRCLES

REAL LIFE SITUATION

PROBLEM SOLVING
DECISION-MAKING
ANALYZING
EVALUATING
CREATING

Quality circles are also discussed in Chapter 5.

Will made two more major changes as he studied his system. He worked with the students to set goals for the next six weeks that would reflect the mission of the class and what quality means to them. The second change was to develop a partnership with the parents. From the parent survey he developed a contract delineating his responsibility for teaching, and the parents' responsibility for creating a positive home climate for learning. Will agreed to let the parents know when major assignments were due, and to help the students with tutoring when needed. He asked the parents to limit TV, allow time for reading at home, and come for at least one conference or visit to the class at least once every twelve weeks.

Will could see some changes in his students, but not many. Yes, they enjoyed class more, and especially the quality circles. But achievement had *not* increased, even though they *were* more cognizant of quality. Oh, well—at least it was a start!

SYSTEM FEEDBACK

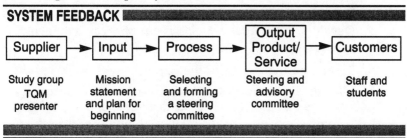

Supplier	Input	Process	Output Product/ Service	Customers
Study group TQM presenter	Mission statement and plan for beginning	Selecting and forming a steering committee	Steering and advisory committee	Staff and students

THE DICKINSON EXPERIENCE

When a study group of Dickinson Independent School District administrators began learning about CIM, the amount of material on quality management was overwhelming and quality gurus were a dime a dozen. Very little of the existing material seemed to meet the specific needs of the school district, however, so the administrators decided to embark on their own search for relevancy. After extensive reading and sorting, the study group primarily focused on the teachings of three authors and practitioners, W. Edwards Deming, William Glasser, and J.M. Juran. In his book *Out of Crisis,* Deming stated his now-famous 14 Points for quality management, which became the subject of intense study for a year by the Dickinson administrators because of their relevancy to public education. Dr. William Glasser is a psychiatrist and long-time practitioner in public schools who has written several books, including *The Quality School.* The Dickinson study group wanted to create a practical synthesis of the two men's work, based on the belief that they complement each other in ways that can benefit public school administrators. The Dickinson group developed four points, or correlates, of quality school management. The study group was able to put the main teachings of Deming, Glasser, and Juran under one of these four correlates. The first one, the subject of this chapter, is summarized as follows:

CORRELATE 1: WORK ON THE SYSTEM

Discussion of quality with students and parents:
1. Defining quality

    a. Quality things in their lives

    b. Quality people in their lives

    c. Quality work and assignments

2. Quality Circles

    a. Open-ended

    b. Diagnostic

    c. Problem-solving

3. Develop with students a classroom Mission Statement:

    a. Work with students to develop student goals

4. Form a partnership with the parents

5. Change the instruction in the class to action learning activities that involve all students and all learning styles.

J. M. Juran's explanation of quality planning and problem-solving tools, in his book *Planning For Quality,* also helped the Dickinson administrators to understand how to harness teams and move toward quality. In later chapters his work will be related to the management of schools.

There are many other writers with excellent ideas on CIM. It is not the authors' intention to exclude anyone, but simply to note that Dickinson administrators focused on the works of the above three authors and practitioners. Too much information, especially at the start of a mind-set shift, can become overwhelming, or at least discouraging. "Keep it simple" were the watchwords as Dickinson educators struggled with the concepts.

In all case histories from industry, a steering committee was formed early in the process to direct the CIM purpose and mission. In several cases more than one steering committee was formed to examine different aspects of CIM. (Large schools may want to do the latter—but, if so, they will still need a central committee to coordinate the activities of the rest.) For example, one large company had the following organization chart in the implementing stage:

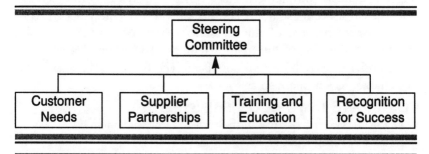

Training and education, both very important functions of the steering committee, will be discussed in Chapter 9. Recognition for success is another important function. The road to quality is hard work, and takes time to travel. The journey will be more enjoyable, and the pitfalls easier to surmount, if celebrations occur when landmarks are reached; a cake with "Congratulations for a Job Well Done" or a full-scale employee gathering are but two of many ways to recognize progress.

Customer feedback is paramount to success as a school embarks on this mission. The business world has made significant progress in listening to its customers. After all, it's hard to eat in a restaurant, or purchase a consumer product, without finding a customer survey as part of the experience. Examining those can give you ideas. The most common forms are:

1. Printed surveys
2. Face-to-face interviews
3. Simulation of being a customer
4. Idea cards/comment cards

Idea cards should be placed throughout the school and community. The card should encourage people to express ideas that will improve quality and cut costs. The ideas should go to the steering committee, where action should be taken on the ideas as soon as possible. A response should be given to the contributor within a week of the date sent. Contributors whose ideas prove to be beneficial should be recognized in some manner. Idea cards in Dickinson have saved time and costs while improving quality in many processes.

MANAGEMENT PRINCIPLES USED
ORGANIZING
1. Form a steering committee from elected and selected faculty members.
2. Include parents who are knowledgeable about CIM.
3. Include at least one community member from a company or industry using CIM.
4. Reflect the ethnicity and different experience levels of the faculty.
5. The size of the steering committee should be 15 percent to 20 percent of the size of the faculty.
6. Encourage the use of a staff advisory committee to experiment with CIM principles.

7. Include all members of the study group who are not part of the steering committee or the advisory committee.
8. Keep membership of the advisory committee open for faculty members accepting the mission of the committee.
9. Decide on a set time, day, and length of any and all committee meetings.

PLANNING

1. Plan an agenda for each meeting. Meetings should be planned to maximize the time allotted.
2. Each meeting should be planned using the following guide:
   a. Set approximate times for items.
   b. Arrange furniture in a circle, to facilitate discussion.
   c. Use visual aids often.
   d. Have at least two easels with poster paper and a variety of colored marking pens available.
   e. Be sure members get the agenda at least two days before the meeting.
   f. Assign someone to keep minutes, especially concerning the decisions made.
   g. Summarize committee actions and decisions at the end of each meeting.
   h. Using a checksheet, have members give feedback on the meeting.
   i. Start on time and end on time.
   j. Stick to the agenda.

CONTROLLING

1. Keep minutes of every meeting, for future reference.
2. Distribute minutes of meetings to everyone in the school, and if feasible to most in the system. Let everyone who should be so informed know what you are doing.

LEADING

1. The principal should either facilitate the steering committee, or delegate it to a trained facilitator.
2. The principal must be a member of the steering committee.
3. The principal may either have final approval of committee decisions, or allow consensus decisions to stand.

Lead Management

W ith its technical name and unique jargon, Continuous Improvement Management can on the surface appear to be such a highly scientific approach to managing organizations that it may leave educators cold. CIM vernacular includes many terms unfamiliar to educators, such as "using tools" to collect data and to reach consensus, and "narrowing the range of variance" in a process. All are important concepts covered later in this book, but for CIM to serve as an adequate framework for producing quality schools, it must have a human face. And because their products are human beings and not inanimate products, schools are human-focused institutions that achieve success only through effective, quality interrelationships between and among individuals.

Producing quality schools, then, depends as much on improving the dynamics of the interactions among the persons associated with the schools as it does on restructuring the planning and decision-making processes of education. Perhaps the business world can learn from emerging Total Quality–managed schools of the 1990s because of this emphasis on the human dimension. The 1970s were marked in America by a corporate push to implement, hodgepodge, a number of features of CIM— namely, quality circles and "worker empowerment." Many companies encouraged, and some trained, employees to discuss and analyze the quality of their products. Teams were formed to investigate ways to improve processes. The missing link: Management structure was never changed to ensure that worker input and decision-making would trickle up to corporate headquarters. At too many companies worker participation was encouraged, but the results of the input either were shelved or never reached the executive suites. Many scholars of management would agree that these efforts failed in part because the corporate world did not attempt to come to grips with the reasons why humans behave as they do, and how a system for interrelationships can be fostered to create a quality work climate.

The examples of Boss and Lead in previous chapters illustrate the contrasting results of opposite styles of management. Boss's coercive system did not allow for meaningful worker participation in decision-making, producing breakdowns in communication and, ultimately, in operations. Lead's system included high levels of worker involvement and effective communication, resulting in a product demanded by customers. Perhaps everyone can think of personal examples of working with or for a Boss; few of us can point to past or present managers we would liken to Lead.

CIM is a collaborative, participatory management system that implies adoption of a lead style of management. There is no place in a Total Quality–managed organization for the strong-arm boss manager. And even if there were, the increasing educational level of the American work force would continue to spell trouble for the boss manager. American workers are too intelligent to blindly follow supervisors—although they may at times appear to conform when they feel they have no choice but to do so outwardly. And the high value that Americans place on personal freedom, which has both advantages and drawbacks in the work place, makes it difficult for boss managers to get subordinates to follow their agendas.

In attempting to improve human interrelationships in order to produce quality schools, the concepts of the aforementioned Dr. William Glasser are helpful. The author of *Reality Therapy* as well as *The Quality School*, Glasser has been an astute observer of schools since the 1970s, as well as an active participant in restructuring education. Control theory, his explanation of why humans behave as they do, explains why CIM can produce quality.

Control theory has as its underlying assumption the idea that we humans choose all of our behaviors, even those that can objectively be judged as destructive or counterproductive. Glasser believes that human behavior focuses around the activities of individuals making decisions and selecting choices that satisfy their wants or needs. We all have the same five basic needs: to survive, to have fun, to experience love and belonging, to have freedom to make choices, and to possess power and receive recognition. All aspects of our behavior can be traced to our desire to fulfill these needs.

Wants and needs are concrete, specific items we develop as pictures in our mind of what we believe is quality in our lives. If actualized, these pictures would fulfill one or more of the five basic needs. Each of us has a quality picture of what we consider fun; whom we consider a caring, loving person; how it feels to belong to another person or other persons; how and where we exercise choices; what it takes to feel powerful; how it feels to receive recognition; and where we are safe and secure.

The daily activities of our lives form a (usually) subconscious process of comparing meaningful situations, relationships, and things with the quality pictures we have affixed in our minds. While we seldom stop to think about it, our mental activities consist of deciding whether a situation, relationship, or thing could satisfy our wants or needs. If there is a match or a near-match, we experience pleasure. If there is not a match, we experience pain. How long the pain lasts depends on what we choose to do. We may simply choose not to do again what caused us pain. However, many times that choice either is not available or may cause more pain if taken. In an effort to reduce the pain, we first do what has worked for us in the past. If repeating the patterns of the past does not work, oftentimes we move on to more creative actions—some of which can appear bizarre to others. (These actions seldom seem extraordinary for us, at least at the time we do them.)

Quality pictures are different for every person; the only common denominator is that all quality pictures are positive, or constructive. However, the choices we make in trying to satisfy these wants or needs can indeed be destructive to us and to others. For example, all students have a need for power. Most elementary students have a picture in their minds of receiving attention from their teachers—recognition, praise, or a few moments of conversation at recess. These pictures are positive and constructive. Envision a boy who chooses a set of behaviors in order to elicit attention from his teacher. He usually will choose behaviors that work in harmony with those of the other students. But say for some reason he does not receive the attention he is seeking. A feeling of dissatisfaction, of the need for power, results. He cannot shut off this need for power, so he begins to control for attention. One day he gets into a fight on the playground, and receives the undivided attention of the teacher as a result. While this isn't the quality attention he wanted, it is better than no attention. Over time, he becomes the playground bully and receives the attention that is due such behavior. Destructive to others and ultimately to him, the bullying nonetheless satisfies a need for power. Until the school helps him to substitute a better choice, he will continue to choose the destructive behavior that he believes will satisfy his needs.

When we get quality in our life, we try to choose behaviors that will repeat the feeling of pleasure we get. We have positive thoughts about the experience and we feel good. We cannot ignore a need. We are always seeking ways to get quality in our lives. When we are not getting enough of a need in our lives, or what we are getting is not close to quality, we must choose a behavior to get back in control. We are constantly trying to control our own lives by satisfying our needs—especially our quality needs.

The prevalence of boss management is easily explained by viewing human behavior through the lens of control theory. Some people have a stronger need than others for power, recognition, and competition. Their need becomes a thirst that diminishes the other basic needs for love, freedom, survival, and fun. Most of their lives are spent satisfying this need for power at the expense of meeting the other needs. When conflicts arise between the need for power and the need for love and belonging, persons such as the classic boss manager choose power-producing behaviors that involve competition and lead to success and recognition. The feelings of belonging and love that come from friends are not as important as the goals that boss managers set, since accomplished goals gain them power.

About 20 percent of all people fall into this category of power-seeking achievers. They normally do well in school because the modern American system of schooling is designed for achievers. Grades, honors, rankings, gold stars, Citizens of the Month awards, and other incentives are designed to recognize the students that teachers view as achievers. What these students do in school is usually not what Glasser would call "quality," but it is good enough to get A's in a system that needs dramatic improvement. When achievers experience failure in school, they usually choose behaviors that overcome the failure. The need for success offsets the feeling of failure. That is not the case with the other needs. Power-seekers do not always choose appropriate behaviors when they experience pain from bad relationships, or when they seek fun or freedom. They have difficulties with leadership roles because they value things rather than relationships. The saying "Power corrupts; absolute power corrupts absolutely" is a pithy commentary on the lives of many achievers who assume leadership positions.

A CASE STUDY OF MANAGEMENT STYLES

Joe's parents always said their firstborn was a born winner. Their memories of him as a student run like a game highlight film, a continuous image of first-place trophies, A+ marks on school work sheets, and star roles in most arenas of performance. Starting in first grade, school was in Joe's view foremost a place where he could outdo his competitors, thus layering positive experiences upon an already solid foundation of self-esteem. He took pride in the fact that he had more gold stars than the other students. He was a competitor, and succeeded in everything he chose to do. He couldn't bear finishing second, so he would do whatever it took to win. By the fifth grade, Joe was doing three to four hours of homework at night. He had begun to set his goals for junior high school, high school, and beyond. He wanted to be an engineer, doctor, or lawyer. They made good money, and money meant prestige and power. While his friends were having fun, Joe was studying. In high school he was a member of three clubs, class treasurer, and an all-sports letter man. Naturally, he was selected as Most Likely to Succeed. SAT scores above 1300 earned Joe acceptance to a prestigious private university. He graduated one semester early with a bachelor's degree in finance. He allowed himself a two-week vacation after graduation, then started in law school—from which he graduated with honors two years later.

By age thirty, Joe had accomplished most of the goals he had identified while in college. His strategy for advancement was simple: Know the right people and perform one notch above the others. He came to realize early in his career that to get to the top he needed to seek out the decision-makers and befriend them with his eagerness and ability. Success for Joe was a formula he had memorized in first grade. Only the circumstances changed as the stakes grew larger. At age forty-two, Joe reached the pinnacle of his career, chief executive officer of his corporation. As a manager he disregarded employee input, and scorned the suggestions of the mid-managers who composed his management team. Since he had few peers with whom to compare himself, Joe believed his decisions were good enough.

One of Joe's productivity ideas was employee work incentives. He called his staff together in the company meeting hall to announce a rigidly structured system by which employees could increase pay by increasing their output. After six months of his incentive plan, he instructed his middle-level managers to fire about 10 percent of the work force, those he considered lazy workers. He set sales-quota goals, and ranked his employees according to their achievement of those quotas. He rewarded the top 50 percent with bonuses, and the top 10 percent were allowed to choose the most lucrative sales territories.

By the time Joe turned fifty, the economy had slipped into a recession and Joe's firm began to lose customers to foreign competition. He blamed everyone else, including the government, for his problems. His reaction to the competition was to place higher quotas on his sales force. Six months later, he laid off more "unproductive" salespersons to cut costs. The bottom line refused to budge and, two years later, Joe was forced by the directors to step down (with an excellent retirement package). His employees lauded him at an elaborate farewell bash, offering tributes through clenched teeth to his "fairness" and "dedication to the American work ethic."

When schools talk about their successes, they are pointing to the Joes of this world—the lawyers, doctors, department managers, engineers, principals, and top-producing sales people whose personalities mirror Joe's. School is designed for this top 20 percent, not the vast majority of students whose internal drives operate in different gears.

After his retirement, Joe took his first "real" vacation in decades, a trip to southern Florida. On the drive south to Miami, he stopped in South Carolina to stay for two days with his younger brother, Dan—his first visit to Dan's home in twenty-two years. Almost an hour into the visit, rummaging through his mind to haul up funny childhood stories to tell, Joe was struck by just how different the two brothers' personalities had always been. As early as he could remember, Dan's world had seemed to revolve around other people, not around achievements. It frustrated Joe to no end when Dan refused to react after losing card games to his older brother.

By first grade, it was obvious that Dan made friends more easily than Joe. He enjoyed recess, story time, talking at lunch, and—most of all—his teacher. He didn't take school very seriously, especially after he developed an opinion that the people at school did not consider him a good reader. He knew this by comparing his reading worksheets with those of his friend Julie, who sat next to him. The teacher never handed Dan and Julie the same worksheet during reading time, and Dan knew who was smarter. After all, Julie had learned to read sentences in kindergarten, and everyone got quiet and listened attentively when she read aloud in class. Dan didn't worry too much about reading, however; he considered his friends, playing at recess, and listening to the radio more enjoyable. He would learn to read when he was ready. Dan's teacher did not use gold stars. She wanted all students to put forth their best efforts, so she encouraged each student with individual comments that Dan eagerly anticipated. Responding to what she perceived as Dan's lack of interest in reading assignments, she allowed him to choose the books he wanted to read.

In third grade, steady encouragement and individual attention by Dan's teachers began to pay dividends. His reading comprehension level increased to grade level over the course of the year. His teacher spent extra time with Dan on writing. She enthusiastically complimented Dan on his ability to express himself in both written and oral form. He could always express himself well with his friends, but now he was getting recognition for it in school. When Dan entered junior high, his outgoing style made him one of the more popular students. He made average grades, but struggled with math. However, his math teacher was patient with him, using games and cooperative groups to make math meaningful and interesting. Dan's friends helped him with math, also.

In high school a teacher took special interest in Dan. She knew he had exceptional interpersonal skills and the ability to express himself well. She encouraged him to try out for the debate team. He not only made the team, but also captured two second-place awards at the district meet. In high school Dan learned a lot, but his grades averaged in the low B's. Dan believed that B's were fine, and felt no pressure to make A's. He excelled in the classes wherein he liked the teacher. He would do quality work for these teachers, "good enough" work for the others. After graduating in the middle of his class, Dan attended junior college for two years, and finished a bachelor's degree in management three years later from the local state college.

After four years of working in several different fields, Dan took a position managing a local office of a national service business. As a manager, he put his employees first on his list of priorities. He made his business an enjoyable yet challenging place to work, constantly asking the staff how they could improve their jobs. He gave his employees the freedom to improve their methods, and encouraged cooperation among workers and between workers and management. Compliance with the rules that had been established under the previous management began to decrease in importance in Dan's office, culminating in the elimination of daily time cards. Dan's employees sensed that he trusted them to be professionals and to do their best on the job. The morale of the office went through the roof, and absenteeism decreased by 50 percent as a consequence.

In his spare time, Dan kept abreast of new management techniques. He studied how best to lead people. Dan was always willing to take a risk if he became convinced it might work. When Continuous Improvement Management articles began to appear in the management trade press, Dan read up on the subject and progressed to books by Deming, Juran, and Glasser. Although he had never heard of these new management theories as a business major in college, the concepts matched how he believed employees should be treated. It also made sense to him that quality could be obtained by trusting workers to continuously improve the quality of their work.

Over the years, Dan's office received every productivity award the company gave. Managers from other branches circulated through his office for training in his management style. When he retired early to launch a second career as a management consultant, it seemed every resident of his town came out to pay tribute. They all said the same thing: Dan walks his talk, and he cares about people before products.

Dan represents the 80 percent of the population that is role-oriented. When given the choice, role-oriented people choose cooperation over competition. Unfortunately, most role-oriented people are forced into competitive work situations where their natural instincts become subverted in the race to survive. They would prefer to satisfy their needs for belonging, caring, fun, and choices over the need for power. While they are as appreciative of recognition as the power-seekers, fulfilling the need for power is secondary to friends, fun, and freedom. If, through caring adults or friends, the need for success is satisfied, role-oriented people will be successful students. They will set goals once they have obtained success in generally noncompetitive ways, usually through genuine relationships with other people.

Some of our best-known leaders are role-oriented. President Bill Clinton fits into this category because of his well-documented need for a steady flow of rapport with other people, his natural friendliness, and his desire to please. Role-oriented people usually become successes or failures as a result of the impact of friends and influential adults. Role-oriented individuals put people before their own goals, seldomly engaging in the quest for power that drives the Joes of the world.

This comparison between the Joes and Dans of the world is only to illustrate the impact of the public schools' tendency to cater to high achievers rather than to role-oriented students. Unless the school provides the caring attention that Dan experienced, role-oriented students run a great risk of losing school from their quality world. When that loss occurs, these students seldom do more than "just get by" in class. In most school systems, 30 percent to 40 percent of the students drop out between the seventh and twelfth grades, and up to 40 percent stay in school but drop out mentally. Only 20 percent of students perform at a quality level in the public schools, and those students invariably are the achievers who can withstand the inspection-oriented system.

Unfortunately for millions of American school children, probably a majority of public schools are in the grips of boss managers, those who adhere to a stimulus–response system of rewards and punishment. They use rules, policies, subjective evaluations, mass inspection, and other forms of coercion to control people's behavior. Boss managers do not believe people can be trusted to do quality work without close supervision and extrinsic rewards (e.g., gold stars). They generally believe that productive behavior comes as a result of law enforcement, and so their daily concerns revolve around what to do to—rather than with—workers and students to get them to behave in an appropriate manner. Of course, the bosses are the ones who determine the appropriate manner. In short, coercion is their mode of operation. The effect on worker behavior is stress and fear.

The top 20 percent of achievers typically perform rather well in boss-managed schools; their self-confidence serves them well in a battle for survival of the fittest. It is difficult to get boss managers to realize that the majority of students and workers are not successful in a stimulus–response environment. When statistics on the number of unsuccessful workers or students are brought to their attention, boss managers typically will claim that the fault lies with the students or workers. Lowering standards or bending the rules will not produce quality, they reply. Instead, students are blamed for not responding to stimulus cues, such as the grades, gold stars, or performance indicators that Joe thrived on. Teachers are blamed for not putting forth the effort to earn whatever stimulus the school offers—incentive pay, good evaluations, and/or the promise of better assignments.

The difference between lead and boss managers is simple: Boss managers do not understand that all people behave in a manner that best satisfies the quality pictures generated in their minds in order to satisfy their needs for survival, love, fun, power, and freedom. All of us have these pictures in our minds, and they become clearer as we grow older. For many, quality pictures for love are spouse, family, friends, and influential people in our lives. We all want to belong, and the easiest way is through cooperation with others. "Fun" quality pictures are those things we do when we do not have to do them. Fishing, golf, sewing, reading for pleasure, listening to music, tennis, and swimming are just a few examples of the behaviors we choose to satisfy our need for fun. Power pictures are those that satisfy our need for recognition, competition, achievement, and attention. Competitive sports are one way we can satisfy the need for power—although many participants in fact do participate in sports with the intention of "having a little fun." For example, many golfers are actually seeking power rather than fun by participating in the sport. That is because they do not achieve satisfaction in the game unless they win, or at least shoot a round that is duly recognized by their peers. For many persons money, a key job position, or an expensive material object (such as a luxury car) are equated with power. These achievers often are the students who fought hardest to get high grades, gold stars, teacher recognition, starting positions on athletic teams, and election to office. Quality pictures of freedom include behaviors that allow us choices, anonymity, and seclusion. We may get freedom in our lives through vacation time, watching a sunset at the beach or mountains, making decisions without interference from others, or any other behavior that results in choices.

Job One for managers in quality schools is to learn that people are never motivated over the long term by external stimuli.

Managers can influence people only by attempting to satisfy their needs and helping them to choose behaviors that fit their best pictures. The success or failure of a school attempting a quality transformation depends on this point. When rules, grades, and evaluations are used to coerce students or workers, they produce at best "good enough" behavior. (When these external motivators are applied, the student or worker perceives them to be coercive.) Since they do not satisfy an internal need, the student or worker chooses behaviors that will produce the least amount of pain; most do just enough work to satisfy the manager. If managers are using external motivators to coerce acceptable behavior, the student or worker eventually will remove work in that environment from his or her best picture album. It is rare that, once a picture is removed, it can be put back again. Quality pictures containing school or work are lost as early as the third grade in schools, or the third month of work for the employee. When elementary school teachers discuss those of their students who seem to be "dropouts in the making," they are referring to students who have removed school from their quality pictures because of the coercive environment.

Persons who desire to be lead managers will fight the boss urge to worship at the altar of rules and regulations. In a sense, rules are the last bastion of order and sense of direction in many American schools. A highly developed code of regulations is perceived in some communities as the hallmark of a quality school—until one questions the students, that is. However, more rules produce only more rule-breaking, and more emphasis on grades produces only more failure. Workers then do not take pride in their work, and workers and students alike are absent for unexplainable reasons. School life then becomes a vicious cycle wherein managers use external stimuli to motivate people who have decided their needs are not being met in the school. The more coercion, the more the students respond with either a "give up" or "get out" attitude. Role-oriented workers and students are the first to begin choosing these behaviors in a non–need-satisfying workplace or classroom. However, even achievers will opt out if their need for power is not satisfied. They will turn that need for power into bullying, coercing peers, and other attention-getting behavior.

In contrast, learning in a noncoercive environment is risk free and meets all of the students' needs. With the use of cooperative groups, learning can enhance the feeling of belonging. A caring teacher will meet students' needs for love and caring, even injecting humor from time to time to satisfy the need for fun. Above all, students must be successful, even if the teacher has to "create" success at the beginning. Students' needs for power will become satisfied through the success they gain in class. If the students are given choices in how they can learn, the classroom experience will satisfy their need for freedom. When students are asked to do quality work in this environment, the chances are good that they will choose that behavior. Learning in a quality classroom is associated with fun, power, cooperation, and choices. If a need-satisfying classroom exists, students will begin to put the teacher in their quality picture albums. Eventually they will put the class subject in their best picture list just as the students in Los Angeles math teacher Jaime Escalante's classes put calculus in their quality world alongside a picture of their teacher.

Lead management is managing in a way so that the workers or students perceive the environment as vital to achieving quality in their lives. When there is trust, the lead manager will model the job or work to be done. The lead manager will ask workers or students how best to do the work. The workers or students will be taught how to assess their own work for quality, and then be allowed to evaluate their work for quality. A lead manager provides the necessary tools.

Lead managers work on the system, while workers/students work in the system. For this reason, the manager is responsible for changing the system to fit the needs of the workers or students. Changing the system means breaking down any barriers that get in the way of quality work. (Of course, asking workers or students is the most accurate way to discover the barriers.) The lead manager solves problems by involving the workers in finding the solutions, oftentimes by working in teams empowered to improve the product or service. When behavior problems occur, the lead manager holds a private conference with the individual to discuss the behavior and reach consensus on how it can be corrected. Punishment is never used, and yet lead managers are neither permissive nor coercive. Instead, work conflicts are solved through two-way communication in a climate of trust.

PRINCIPAL PAT ANN HOLD

The steering committee facilitated by Pat had received training in the following areas:

1. Understanding the school as a system and identifying suppliers, inputs, processes, outputs, and customers
2. Utilizing the principles of lead management
3. Conducting effective meetings.

The committee conducted an awareness inservice on CIM principles for the Trail's End faculty. They began planning how to accomplish the mission statement, but only after first recognizing the defects and waste in the system. Committee members gathered data that might indicate possible defects in the system. This work led the committee to realize the need for structural changes in the system designed to eliminate barriers to continuous improvement and quality. The committee members believed the school should concentrate on improving customer satisfaction. This meant that everyone needed to begin discussions with their customers to discover needs. Last, but not least, the committee wanted to recognize those contributing to quality and celebrate their successes.

Under Pat's guidance the steering committee decided to form five working groups to prepare for the move to continuous improvement through CIM. One group would be responsible for system changes. A second would evaluate customer satisfaction. The third group would determine continuous improvement goals. The fourth group would concentrate on developing training plans for the staff. The last group would examine ways to recognize staff members who are successful in using quality principles. The committee as a whole would be involved in developing an introductory plan for CIM in the school. The advisory committee would begin experimenting with noncoercive management of classrooms, using lead management principles.

The group responsible for system changes decided to focus on major barriers, such as how to change the grading system to reduce the reliance on grades as a measure of quality; how to make the curriculum more relevant; how to measure quality through subject competency and skills mastery rather than tests, credits, and time-based promotions; how to organize the school around customers instead of subjects; and how to use teams for continuous improvement.

The group decided it would need to seek input from the staff regarding structural barriers that keep Trail's End from eliminating defects and waste, and from satisfying the needs of customers. Structural barriers are impediments that can be changed through policy revision and reorganization. Once structural barriers are identified, the committee must develop criteria of what the school would look like without the barrier. Using the criteria, the committee should benchmark schools that exhibit the criteria successfully.

The customer satisfaction group developed a survey to determine student satisfaction with the process of learning. The survey was designed to reflect the degree to which Trail's End Middle School helped students to achieve the basic needs as identified by Glasser. Results would be shared with the staff. In addition, the school contracted with a firm to administer and analyze a survey of the organizational health of the school from the staff's perspective. The information would be used by the steering committee to plan for improving the work climate of the school. The group realized that, until the school had an acceptable health level, getting change to happen would be difficult.

The group studying continuous improvement goals selected a system that would gauge the current situation while recording the progress in reducing defects and waste. Setting goals, such as a 10 percent reduction in a defect or 20 percent increase in test scores, is an example of classic short-term thinking. Once the goal is achieved, usually no effort is made to carry the goal to its next logical plane. When a school focuses on short-term goals, it usually begins to use quick fixes that are costly and not necessarily effective in the long run. Emphasis on short-term goals can cause workers and managers to reach the desired numbers at all costs, even using dishonest or wasteful methods.

Performance Goal Indexing (PGI) is a better approach, since it incorporates criteria selected by the staff as measurements of quality. By plotting the progress of the indicators on a 1000-point scale, the staff can get a clear idea of the progress being made at the school. Because it embraces the concept of continuous improvement rather than short-term goal-setting, PGI helps the manager and workers look at the long term. Solutions can be carefully and systematically developed over a period of time.

The performance goal committee should include parents and business/community leaders. The committee should get input from the staff and students as to what criteria are considered important as indicators of quality for the school. Typical performance criteria would be test scores, attendance, number of serious discipline problems, and number of retentions. The criteria should be used to set continuous improvement goals, using the performance index format. The results should be presented to the faculty periodically. The graph of the index should be displayed on school bulletin boards and in the school newsletters. The faculty and parents should be able to see the progress of the school toward quality. Continuous improvement is indicated by a steady movement upward in the line graph from an index of 300 to 1000. The procedure for constructing a performance goal index is explained at the end of this chapter.

The group responsible for training began by looking at the first two correlates of CIM—Work on the system, and Adopt the principles of lead management. After gathering samples of training materials on these areas from other school districts using CIM and from industry, the group set about the task of developing training modules for the staff.

The recognition group began looking for ways to publicize the individual successes of teachers who were implementing CIM principles. A newsletter, *Quality Corner*, featuring teachers' quality ideas, was published each month. Recognition at the school board, personal notes to individuals using the quality principles, pizza parties to recognize success, and many other ideas were brainstormed by the committee.

Pat felt confident that the working groups would help turn the corner in introducing CIM to the staff. The voice of instinct told her, however, that the single most important factor in winning over the staff would be her ability to be a lead manager. She ticked off a number of activities she should become involved in as a daily part of her commitment to lead management: Modeling instruction by going into the classroom to teach, further expanding her open-door policy, giving the staff choices and input into decisions. Building trust would be the goal. Only when the leaders practiced lead management would staff members adopt lead management principles in the classroom. Instead of doing things to or for people, Pat began doing things with people. She set aside 25 percent of her time for MWWA—that is, Management While Wandering Around. As she became reacquainted with parts of the school, she astounded her staff with such questions as: "What do we need to do to improve?" "What are you doing that is working?" and "What does quality mean to you?"

TEACHER WILL E. SURVIVE

The quality circle meetings were starting to pay dividends as students began to see the difference between "good enough" work and quality. Will selected a writing assignment to allow students to test their ideas about quality. As a class, the students brainstormed the criteria that would be used to judge for quality. The class then rated some writing assignments from the previous year, using their criteria. The papers rated as quality by the students were placed on the bulletin board as models. The students did a better job of writing than in the past. A few even met the criteria for quality. Will decided to allow students to do rework after one student told him he could have improved his paper after seeing the quality of the others. Will began to allow any student to improve his or her grade by reworking it at home. He would change the grade if the quality of the paper improved. Several students took him up on this innovation. He decided to continue the practice by using it with major assignments. "Continuous improvement to reach quality" became the guiding principle in his class.

Will recognized he had a mixture of achievers and role-oriented students in his class. The achievers were the ones who consistently completed homework. They were always asking what was going to be on the test. They did not like to work in cooperative groups because they did not like sharing knowledge; they complained that they did most of the work. Achievers resisted any activity that did not create clearly defined winners and losers. The role-oriented students, on the other hand, enjoyed working in groups. They were always asking questions, such as "Why are we studying this?" or "What is the purpose for this?" When an assignment seemed relevant to them, they would do quality work. Otherwise, they would produce just enough to pass. Will also recognized that he had a few of what he termed failure-oriented students. They sat in the back of the room and worked hard at being noticed and living up to their role as a failure. For them, homework was an impossibility. And paper-and-pencil tests were rarely completed; they gave up before the others got started.

Will used his knowledge of lead management to try to satisfy the needs of all his students. The achievers needed to learn cooperative skills. He assigned them roles as leaders of groups, and gave them extra credit based on how well they achieved cooperation in their group. He constantly encouraged them to continuously improve their work until it was quality. With role-oriented students he made special attempts to make the assignment relevant, making it a point to state contemporary uses for the skills and facts they were acquiring. He asked the class for input in determining what was important to know in each unit. He began developing units around themes to provide contextual meaning. And he incorporated more field trips and labs to make learning relevant. The failure-oriented students were the toughest to reach. He met individually with each student, to build trust. He asked them for advice and gave them choices. Above all, he created success for them. He broke down tasks into smaller parts which they would be more successful, and he made sure there was some fun involved in each lesson. Some were even beginning to trust him enough to do work in class. All this was quite an achievement, since most of the failure-oriented students had not done any school work in years.

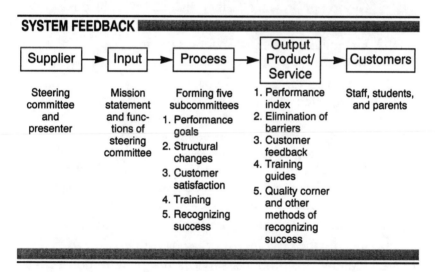

PERFORMANCE GOAL INDEXING

Performance goal indexing gives an organization an inexpensive, versatile, and powerful tool. The indicators are easily read, and visually identify the impact of change. The process assists the group in clarifying goals and reviewing the organization's mission. PGI is useful as a continuous improvement measure. There are no set goals for monthly, quarterly, or annual targets. Rather, the focus is on continuous improvement of performance until the index is close to 1000. At that time the index needs to be reproduced with new goals.

PGI provides insights into current levels of performance and tracks the performance of the organization through time. Above all, it focuses the organization's improvement efforts so that it finds the important items to work on. Since quality schools rely on measurement to make decisions about process improvement, a reliable, appropriate system for gathering that data should be developed. PGI recognizes that:

- Measurement is a tool of good management
- A system for indicating trends promotes excellence
- The best measures are designed by workers or line managers
- Results should be used primarily to improve the process, and secondarily to report improvement

PGI combines a family of measures into one comprehensive number, using:

- Group performance (rather than that of individuals)
- Indications of performance trends
- A common numerical scoring system
- Weight factors

PGI captures the essential characteristics of quality, timeliness, and cost effectiveness. It serves as a score card, providing a common number on which to concentrate efforts. The following are the steps toward developing and using PGI.

Step 1: Describe the System and Define the Mission

The first step should be to document what the organizational unit does, and define or review its mission.

a. Whom is the organization established to serve?

b. Identify the customer/user needs.

c. Identify the products/services the organization produces to satisfy customer/user needs. What are the organization outputs?

d. Review answers to a, b, and c with your customers, and make the necessary adjustments.

e. Identify the principal resources (labor, supplies, energy, raw materials, capital) used by the organization to produce these products/services. What are the inputs?

f. Describe what people do in the organization in order to produce products/services.

g. Finally, in no more than one paragraph, describe the mission of the organization.

Step 2: Select Key Performance Indicators

Performance measures usually are defined in terms of a ratio or fraction, but can be a discrete number. Every department or organization must develop its own indicators. Three to seven well-chosen ones will suffice to measure performance. In general, each indicator needs to be thoroughly defined and the sources specifically identified to ensure reliable results. Make sure the chosen key performance indicators:

- Are easily identifiable

- Have readily available data which preferably are being collected

- Measure service performed rather than easily countable activities

- Are developed with a purpose in mind, e.g., identifying opportunities for improvement

- Are simple to understand

- Account for variation in inflation and/or energy in both denominator and numerator to the same degree, i.e., constant dollar terms

Measurements should focus on improving each of the following areas:

a. **Quality** (conformance to requirements). Quality measures effective use of resources, satisfaction of customers, and the needs of the school. Various survey techniques can be used to assess the level of your customers' satisfaction.

b. **Cost effectiveness** (quantity produced at the least possible cost). Cost effectiveness measures efficient use of resources. Assess how well the resources of labor, energy, capital, and materials are being used to provide products/services to your customers. Productivity is included in cost effectiveness.

c. **Timeliness.** This measures delivery of the department's products and/or services. Examples are:

1. Claims per week

2. Test scores per year

3. Student attendance per grading period

4. Retentions per year

5. Customer survey results (5-point scale)

An example of performance indicators for improvement of math are:

Campus/Department — Math				
Performance Indicators	% Failures/ 6 wks	% Students higher math	Students liking math/ 5 pt scale	9th grade state tests

Step 3: Establish Current Performance Levels

The current performance level for each indicator is usually based upon an average of three months or more of data collected from existing or historical records. Data must be cost effective; the cost of collecting data should not be higher than the expected benefits. If no data are available, make the best possible subjective estimation of the current performance levels, or consider another indicator.

As the example shows, these levels are always entered in the boxes corresponding to the score of 3 in the matrix. This allows future performance levels greater room for improvement, and for declines on the 0–10 rating scale.

Campus/Department — Math				
Performance Indicators	% Failures/ 6 wks	% Students higher math	Students liking math/ 5 pt scale	9th grade state tests
Current Performance	12.60%	6.30%	3.2	64% MASTERY
10				
9				
8				
7				
6				
5				
4				
3 (current)	12–12.9	6.0–7.9	3.1-3.2	61–65

Step 4: Establish Goals

Set realistic goals that the organization wishes to achieve. Goals defined as percentages can be optimistic. Perfection is sometimes won, for example, with 100 percent on-time deliveries and zero defects. Much discussion and good judgment will be required to select the right goals for this, the highest performance level.

The goals are entered in the matrix at the level corresponding to the score of 10.

Campus/Department — Math				
Performance Indicators	% Failures/ 6 wks	% Students higher math	Students liking math/ 5 pt scale	9th grade state tests
Current Performance	12.60%	6.30%	3.2	64% MASTERY
10 (Desired goals)	BELOW 6%	20+%	ABOVE 4.4	ABOVE 95%
9				
8				
7				
6				
5				
4				
3	12–12.9	6.0–7.9	3.1-3.2	61–65

Step 5: Establish Minigoals

The intermediate performance levels 4 to 9 can be thought of as minigoals. Each succeeding score should be meaningful to the preceding one and define progress toward the ultimate goal. In the absence of other considerations, a linear scale is used. That is, the numerical distance from each intermediate score to the next is the same.

The minigoals are entered into the matrix at the levels corresponding to the scores of 4, 5, 6, 7, 8, and 9.

Step 6: Establish Lower Performance Levels

Determine the minimum performance levels below which it is unlikely that the organization will fall. Enter them in the matrix at the level corresponding to the score of 0. Accounting for occasional slack periods and tradeoffs, determine a scale of performance levels corresponding to the scores of 1 and 2.

These are entered in the boxes corresponding to the scores of 0, 1, and 2.

Campus/Department — Math				
Performance Indicators	% Failures/ 6 wks	% Students higher math	Students liking math/ 5 pt scale	9th grade state tests
Current Performance	12.60%	6.30%	3.2	64% MASTERY
10 (Desired goals)	BELOW 6%	20+%	ABOVE 4.4	ABOVE 95%
9	6–6.9	18–19.9	4.3–4.4	91.95
8	7–7.9	16–17.9	4.1–4.2	86–90
7	8–8.9	14–15.9	3.9–4.0	81–85
6	9–9.9	12–13.9	3.7–3.8	76–80
5	10–10.9	10–11.9	3.5–3.6	71–75
4	11–11.9	8.0–9.9	3.3–3.4	66–70
3	12–12.9	6.0–7.9	3.1–3.2	61–65
2	13–13.9	4.0–5.9	2.9–3.0	56–60
1	14–14.9	2.0–3.9	2.7–2.8	50–55
0	ABOVE 14	BELOW 2.0	BELOW 2.7	BELOW 50%

Step 7: Assign Weights

In order to combine the indicators into one overall index number, each indicator is given a weighted numerical value that represents relative importance. The sum of these weights must equal 100. This is a crucial step. Deciding the relative importance defines how quality and productivity improvement fit together in the mission of the organization. Assigning weights is subjective. A consensus of the team is required, and a farsighted view is needed.

The weight of each key performance indicator is entered in the appropriate box on the weight row.

Campus/Department — Math				
Performance Indicators	% Failures/ 6 wks	% Students higher math	Students liking math/ 5 pt scale	9th grade state tests
WEIGHT	20	35	20	25

Step 8: Tabulate Scores and Calculate Index

After all adjustments are verified and completed, make these results of steps 2–7 the final action plan. From now on, the base of the matrix must not be changed during a calendar year because comparisons between periods would become meaningless. Annually you may want to revise the matrix to best describe the current conditions. At the conclusion of each monitoring period, gather the data and plot the results (monthly, quarterly, or annual.)

a. The actual measure for each key performance indicator is calculated and entered on the performance line of the matrix.

b. The actual performance for each indicator is circled on the matrix. If a minigoal is not attained, circle the lower performance level. Any performance worse than the 0 score would still receive a 0. Likewise, any score greater than 10 would still receive a 10.

A performance goal index for three periods follows.

Campus/Department — Math				
Performance Indicators	% Failures/ 6 wks	% Students higher math	Students liking math/ 5 pt scale	9th grade state tests
1993	5.60	8.90	3.3	78% MASTERY
1992	10.2	7.30	3.6	60% MASTERY
Benchmark 1991	12.60%	6.30%	3.2	64% MASTERY
10	BELOW 6	20+%	ABOVE 4.4	ABOVE 95%
9	6–6.9	18–19.9	4.3–4.4	91.95
8	7–7.9	16–17.9	4.1–4.2	86–90
7	8–8.9	14–15.9	3.9–4.0	81–85
6	9–9.9	12–13.9	3.7–3.8	76–80
5	10–10.9	10–11.9	3.5–3.6	71–75
4	11–11.9	8.0–9.9	3.3–3.4	66–70
3	12–12.9	6.0–7.9	3.1–3.2	61–65
2	13–13.9	4.0–5.9	2.9–3.0	56–60
1	14–14.9	2.0–3.9	2.7–2.8	50–55
0	ABOVE 14	BELOW 2.0	BELOW 2.7	BELOW 50%
Score for 1993	10	4	4	6
Weight	20	35	20	25
Value (score x weight)	200	140	80	150

Year/Month	1991	1992	1993
Index	300	330	570
1993 Index=	570		

A graph of the index would show continuous improvement toward their goals in the math department.

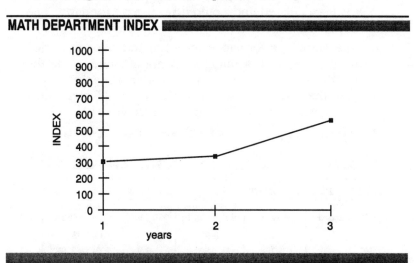

MATH DEPARTMENT INDEX

THE DICKINSON EXPERIENCE

One effective method for managers to measure the perceptions of the workers under their leadership is the organizational health perception survey. The Dickinson Independent School District uses a commercial survey called the Organizational Health Inventory (OHI) developed in and normed from over 1,000 companies. Dr. Marvin Fairman developed the tool while teaching at the University of Arkansas. In Dickinson, the fifty-item survey is administered to each school and department staff, including the central office, after the spring break. The survey measures ten variables for organizational health:

1. Distribution of power

2. Vertical and horizontal communication

3. Goal focus

4. Morale

5. Cohesiveness

6. Autonomy of the worker

7. Problem-solving ability

8. Adaptation of the organization to outside influences

9. Utilization of the talents of the staff

10. Innovation

After the data are analyzed and normed, a profile for each work unit is created on graphs. The strengths and weaknesses of the organization are discussed by sharing the results of the OHI survey with the staff. Then the manager (or management team) determines one or more variables as the focus for improvement during the year. Without the possibly coercive presence of the manager, the staff brainstorms problems and possible solutions associated with the leader, the followers, and the structure of the organization. Solutions are presented to the management team whose purpose now is to develop an action plan to improve both the variable(s) and the overall organizational health.

MANAGEMENT PRINCIPLES USED

ORGANIZING

1. Establish five subcommittees to handle special functions of the steering committee.
2. Plan as a committee of the whole.
3. Organize subcommittees to include other staff members, parents, community members, and even students in secondary schools.

PLANNING

1. Plan an agenda for each meeting to maximize use of time.
2. Include reports from the subcommittees on each agenda.

CONTROLLING

1. Develop a performance index for the school.
2. Publicize the performance index, so that all can keep track of the continuous progress toward quality.
3. Conduct Organizational Health Inventory and analyze profiles.

LEADING

CORRELATE 2: ADOPT LEAD MANAGEMENT PRINCIPLES.

Principal must model lead management by:

1. Building trust.

2. Providing and promoting a caring, enjoyable, risk-free climate within the school.

3. Eliminating fear by removing coercion as a means of motivating others. (This means reducing the reliance on grades, rankings, summative tests, and subjective evaluations as inspection tools.)

4. Breaking down barriers to cooperative efforts and to continuous improvement for quality.

5. Asking workers and students for their input into decisions affecting them.

6. Facilitating and coaching others to adopt lead management principles.

7. Beginning collection of data from all parts of the system (input, processes, and output), in order to base evaluations and decisions on data, rather than on opinions.

8. Providing training and education for all in lead management principles, control theory, and reality therapy.

Self-Assessment of Quality

Boss, the leader of the ill-fated wagon train, used mass inspection, rankings, and averages to achieve quality control. Rather than trust his workers to determine the best way to get the job done, he used fear, inspection, and competition to get them to do it his way. The result was the breakdown of two-way communication between the workers and Boss. Without feedback, Boss operated in the dark, basing his actions on instinct rather than on knowledge from those closest to the processes he tried desperately to control. When confronted with defects, Boss recycled the product through the same inefficient system. His inspection process was in reality inspection after the fact; the defective products had used materials that were now waste. The product had to be redone, when it could have been produced right the first time.

Lead, the wagon master of the quality wagon train, trusted his workers to assess the quality of their own work. He knew that those closest to the problems understood better than anyone else how to evaluate processes and to produce quality. Lead provided workers with job-specific training and gave them the information they needed to assess their own work. In return they willingly provided Lead with information that he needed to assess the progress made to improve processes.

Boss is not different from managers today who use rankings, averages, evaluations, grading, and mass inspection of the product to control for quality. Ranking workers or students still produces a few winners and a majority of losers. The fallacy of ranking is seen in the fact that one can get ahead only when others falter. In a group of 100 schools ranked by state test scores, there always will be fifty whose performance ranks above average and fifty whose performance ranks below average. A school with improving scores might still rank low if the other schools' scores also improve. Thus, such a ranking system cannot reflect individual improvement, which is a truer measure of quality than is comparison with a disparate whole. Further, in a competitive environment produced by ranking systems, there is no motivation to share ideas for the good of everyone. Schools use these destructive systems when they rank teachers for merit pay, and rank students by using such mass inspection methods as state and national norm–referenced tests. Because they always produce sets of losers, inspection and ranking are not helpful way stations on the route to quality.

Boss managers also use subjective evaluation methods and grading, ostensibly to spur improvement. In reality these coercive devices produce nothing more than fear. Evaluations are at best the self-oriented opinions of a supervisor who has not experienced the unique situation faced by the person being evaluated. Antagonism toward the supervisor, based on a perception of an unfair evaluation, far outstrips any "constructive" criticism (there is no such thing) that any boss could offer. Schools cannot continue to have winners and losers. To compete in a global economy, American schools need to produce only winners—every teacher and every student. Schooling is not a game. Competition in education should be the domain of fun-generating activities, such as athletics, and not of something as vital as learning. Cooperation is the only way that all students can achieve quality.

Allowing workers or students to assess their own quality is the first step toward establishing a cooperative rather than competitive system. Schools that have implemented self-assessment have found that employees and students assume a high degree of responsibility for their work, often for the first time. There is something innately pleasing about being able to determine one's own strengths and weaknesses, and to have a role in planning for improvement. Self-assessment does not work in a vacuum, of course and supervisors who have been trained as lead managers can more effectively than others conference with workers or students to validate the self-assessments and point out ways to improve. Rather than coercion, the supervisor shows workers or students that they are on the team. The adversarial relationship then evaporates in a new atmosphere of trust.

TOOLS TO ASSESS QUALITY

Before workers are allowed to assess their own quality, they must learn how to identify defects and waste in their processes, and how to monitor a process for quality. Defects can be defined as any excessive deviations from the norm. All processes have some degree of variation in the outputs; even in automated manufacturing processes, there is a minute degree of variation in each fabricated part. Variation in the schools occurs, for example, when a physical-education teacher charts the time it takes participating students to run from one end of the playground to the other. An elementary school teacher would find variation in any number of processes, from the number of spelling mistakes on student papers to the number of months it takes students to learn to read a sentence.

CHECK SHEETS

Either teacher could make a study of variation by recording each student's performance on a check sheet. Check sheets are a key tool in collecting and organizing data, since they can record where the problem is occurring, its frequency, and often the source of the variation. To use a check sheet effectively, the data collector first must identify:

1. The type of data to be collected
2. How the data will be acquired, i.e., counted, measured
3. What period will be covered, i.e., one week, month, or quarter
4. Who will collect the data

There are three common types of check sheets:

Recording Check Sheet

This check sheet is used to depict measured or counted data. It normally requires making only tick marks.

The check sheet may be as general or as specific as necessary. For instance, instead of just showing the total occurrences, it can be modified to show occurrences by person, by week, for each day of the week, etc.

PROBLEM	MARK EACH TIME IT OCCURS
Copy machine jams	ЖЖ ЖЖ III

Check List Check Sheet

This check list simply lists the various tasks that must be done in the format of a grocery shopping list. It is used to ensure that all tasks have been completed. A group might use this check sheet when assigning research areas to members, in attempting to solve problems.

Problem/Defect Location Check Sheet

These check sheets are used to collect data on occurrences. They are usually pictures, illustrations, or graphs, with tick marks made on them as the problem/defect occurs. A data collector attempting to find a solution to on-the-job injuries might make a rough diagram of the property layout, and place a check mark at each location for each injury sustained.

HISTOGRAMS

Once data is collected on the frequency of an occurrence in a process, histograms can be used to show whether the process has a normal distribution. *Histograms are pictorial graphs of process variation.* By studying the graph it can be determined whether the variation is normal or erratic. Normal variation can be reduced over a period of time through collective efforts, while erratic variation demands immediate special attention.

A *normal* distribution exists when the variation in a process is random. Random variation is what one might statistically expect to occur given the particular system. Nonrandom or *erratic* variation should be investigated because it occurs for unexpected reasons. It does not mean the cause is necessarily bad, but that at the very least *something* is influencing the process. A good use for histograms is teacher grade distributions. The example on page 59 outlines steps in constructing a histogram.

Plotting histograms of grade distributions will help teachers gain insight into the learning process. Note that the histogram of the accompanying grade distribution on page 60 is not a bell-shaped figure, thus signifying that the variations in the grades are not random. The *double-peaked* distribution of this histogram indicates that probably two distinct processes are at work. In other words, the teacher may be using a method of instruction that is processed differently by two groups of students. This is common when teachers predominantly use lectures that auditory learners process well, but visual and tactile kinesthetic learners do not.

GRADE DISTRIBUTION OF 120 STUDENTS

75	65	84	72	95	88	68	63	94	72	92	90
93	50	70	71	64	91	65	93	71	94	73	92
62	99	68	92	63	72	72	97	72	69	71	69
68	93	72	91	71	74	73	72	77	68	94	71
70	69	71	74	97	95	75	68	90	82	90	78
95	89	93	86	55	77	83	99	91	95	72	82
94	92	94	87	54	78	90	58	81	94	93	93
88	93	80	97	60	96	90	73	72	71	92	91
90	71	82	98	92	95	70	84	73	73	93	65
61	85	63	96	89	93	60	96	68	95	71	68

1. Rank the data from high to low

2. Determine the range (the difference) between the highest and lowest scores. Since the highest number is 99 and the lowest is 50, the range is 49.

3. Determine the bars needed. If the number of measurements is under 50 use 5 to 7 bars. For 51 to 100 measurements use 6 to 10 bars, 101 to 250 use 7 to 12 bars and over 250 measurements use 10 to 20. Since the example has 120 measurements, there is a choice between seven and 12 bars. For this example 10 bars will be selected.

4. Determine the span of the individual bars necessary to divide the measurement range into equal parts. Divide the range by the number of bars to get the span. If the range is 49 and the number of bars is 10, then the span is 4.9. Rounding off each bar is 5 points wide.

5. Construct a Bar Table. Count the number of occurrences or data points in each bar's range. This number, the frequency of the measurement, is the height of the bar.

INTERVAL	FREQUENCY
50–55	3
56–60	3
61–65	9
66–70	13
71–75	27
76–80	5
81–85	8
86–90	12
91–95	31
96–100	9

6. Plot the histogram. Number of occurrences (frequency) vs. measurements (bar boundaries).

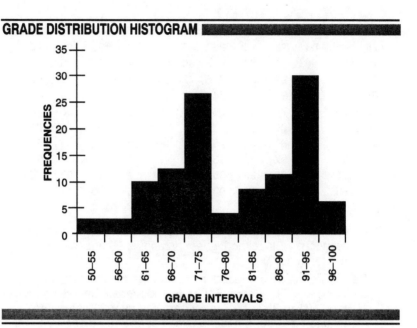

GRADE DISTRIBUTION HISTOGRAM

FREQUENCIES (y-axis): 0, 5, 10, 15, 20, 25, 30, 35

GRADE INTERVALS (x-axis): 50–55, 56–60, 61–65, 66–70, 71–75, 76–80, 81–85, 86–90, 91–95, 96–100

A second common shape for a histogram is the *skewed* distribution. If the teacher's instruction is having a positive effect on learning, then the distribution will skew to the positive side. If the instruction is skewed to the negative side, it is possible that there is an undesirable influence upon the process. Teachers plotting histograms of the grades of their students can get good insights into the kinds of learning that occur at a random frequency. As teachers using CIM methods with effective strategies work with students, the distribution of grades should become skewed positively as the average moves toward the limit of 100.

CONTROL CHARTS

Another statistical tool that schools can use to help find variation in a process is the control chart. A control chart is a line graph of data points with upper and lower limits. The upper and lower limits are the most distant points in a normal random distribution. These points are three sigmas, or standard deviations, from the average, which means that 99.73 percent of all data points should be within the upper and lower control limits. According to statistical probability, there is only one chance in 400 that a data point would exist outside the three sigma limits. Points that fall outside the upper and lower limits are called *special causes*. A special cause is excessive variance. Control charts are important because they delineate between common causes, which are those data points that fall within the upper and lower control limits, and special causes, which fall outside the limits.

For purposes of improving processes, it is important to understand that common causes are the result of the system, and therefore are not the particular responsibility of the individual worker. Common causes could be poor equipment, ineffective procedures, inferior materials, or "other," all controlled by management. Special causes fall outside of the range that is considered normal, and thus are within the individual worker's control. Special causes could be machinery breakdown, worker error, freaks of nature, or other explainable causes known by the worker.

When managers observe a special cause, they should find the reasons for it by asking the workers. The workers also should be allowed to fix the problem, if indeed a fix is required. Oftentimes the special cause represents a fluke occurrence, and can be ignored once explained. If the special cause is positive, then management should find out if it can be duplicated to help improve the process. However, many positive special causes are data errors (or manipulations of the data). Approximately 7 percent of all causes are special causes in most processes. All other data points within the limits are common causes, which are the responsibility of management, and in no way the workers, to correct. This is because workers work in the system; managers work on it.

Common causes cannot be addressed until the process is in control. It is out of control until all special causes are explained or corrected. Once the process is in control, correcting common causes will allow the average to improve, forming new upper and lower limit points. Management improves common causes by organizing the workers to improve their process, an advance that can be accomplished both by allowing workers to keep their own control charts, thus giving them access to necessary information, and by trusting them to make progress.

There are numerous types of control charts, only one of which—*average charts*—will be explained in this book. Manufacturing and industrial quality process control personnel can explain other types of control charts. The type of control chart that should be used depends on the type of data that will be charted. The key to understanding control charts is that the upper and lower control limits reflect the limits of random occurrence. Any data that occurs *outside* the limits could not statistically occur by chance. For example, a chart of student absences over 36 weeks might look like the following. The upper control limit (UCL) and lower control limit (LCL) are three sigmas, or standard deviations, from the average. To figure the control limits, the average of the data points must first be calculated. The average is the sum of the student absences divided by the number 36, which is 64 in this example. Control limits are calculated using the following formula:

UCL = Average plus (+) 3 times the square root of the average
LCL = Average minus (–) 3 times the square root of the average

For this example, the upper limit is calculated as 64 + 3 × the square root of 64. The lower limit is calculated as 64 – 3 × the square root of 64. Three times the square root of 64 (8) is 24. The upper control limit, then, is 64 + 24, or 88 student absences. The lower control limit is 64 – 24, or 40 student absences per week.

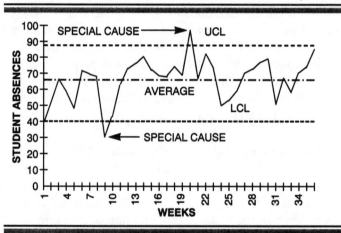

Although control charts help in understanding the degree of variation in a process, it is not necessary to understand them in order to implement CIM. There are many computer programs that can create control charts using input data. Everyone should understand the concepts that control charts illustrate, and most particularly the relationship between special causes and common causes. To reiterate, data points that fall within the upper and lower control limits are common causes, meaning they are the expected results of the system. Data points that are outside of the upper and lower control limits are special causes, and not the result of random occurrence. Managers too often commit judgment errors because they do not distinguish between the two types of causes. These mistakes fall into one of two categories: tinkering and tampering.

Tinkering occurs when a special cause is treated like a common cause. If data indicate that a worker has excessive cause beyond the control limits, the worker is a special cause. If management calls a meeting of all employees to announce a new tardy policy because of that worker's infractions, management has treated a special cause as a common cause—that is, a cause common to all workers. Since most workers have stayed within an acceptable range of variation in tardiness, the new policy seems to them to make no sense. Trust erodes therefore, and eventually the quality of work deteriorates. Management could have avoided these problems by having a conference with the worker whose tardies were out of control.

The second mistake, *tampering*, occurs when a common cause is treated as a special cause. For example, boss managers often rank workers as above average or below average in performance. The rewards for performing above average may be grades, gold stars, money, promotions, special bonuses, nice offices, or extra privileges. However, through control charting it becomes clear that, statistically, *all* performance levels that fall between the upper and control limits are common, expressing insignificant variance. To rank from the criterion of above or below average makes no sense statistically. The emphasis should be on raising the average and, therefore, the upper and lower control limits, by enlisting all workers' help in improving the process. Instead, boss managers treat each worker as a special cause, blaming those below average and rewarding those above average. Tampering pits worker against worker in competition for the available awards. Quality suffers because the fact that 50 percent of workers will always be below average under this system creates a natural barrier to improvement.

To begin using histograms and control charts, the process owner needs to adhere to the following sequence. First, a process to measure must be identified. The process owner should create a flow diagram to understand the activities and decision points in the process. (Flow diagraming will be described in the next chapter.) The flow diagram will indicate the best stages in the process at which to collect data. Once the process is understood, the type of data and the measurement tool to use should be decided. Histograms and control charts can be used to measure defects, waste, or variance in data that may indicate excessive deviation.

Defect measurement requires a standard set by management. For example, if a standard for grades is set at C or better, then D's and F's are defects, and can be charted or displayed on a histogram. Errors in typing, complaints, accidents, discipline problems, and dropouts are a few examples of process outputs that are classified as defects because they do not meet a standard.

Waste measurement is the measurement of inputs versus outputs, whether of materials, cost, or time. To measure the waste, the amount of input material can be compared with that of the output material. The waste can be charted over time, to discover whether or not the process is in control. The cost of the input plus the cost of the process can be compared with the value placed on the output (or a standard) to determine waste in costs. If the cost of inputting and processing an insurance claim is $247 and the standard set by the insurance company is $165, then the waste is $82. To determine waste over a time period, the time required to move an input through a process can be measured against a standard. This too can be charted or diagramed, using a histogram to determine variation, special causes, and common causes.

Besides those of defects and waste, measurements can be made of the outputs of any other process to check for *excessive variance* and possible problems. Teacher class grades, student absences, individual student grades, discipline cases by teachers, and time required to complete grade reports are but a few outputs for which statistical process tools (SPC) tools can be used.

Of course, teaching workers the tools they need to assess their own quality will have no impact on continuous improvement, in the absence of a lead manager. Trust must be present between worker and management for the improvement to occur. Trust cannot be obtained through the use of subjective employee evaluations, ranking workers or students, or setting short-term goals or quotas, or even grades. It requires training of all personnel in the use of SPC tools. Management must provide the necessary information for process owners to have the data to use in the SPC charts and diagrams. Management also must empower the worker by delegating authority to correct common and special causes in their processes. Management further must give workers the resources they need to solve the problems. When management owns the process, special causes need to be corrected by conferring with the workers. Management is responsible for common causes, and so should not only organize and provide the resources that the workers need to reduce the common causes, but should also act on the system to eliminate barriers that inhibit communication vertically and horizontally across the system, and other barriers that deprive workers of their pride of workmanship. Only management can act on the system to improve quality.

PRINCIPAL PAT ANN HOLD

Pat was enthusiastic about allowing people to assess their own quality, but she was daunted by the fact that SPC tools take some time to learn, let alone to apply to real-life situations. She also knew the training group was working hard to master the tools so they could create training based on them. In the meantime, Pat decided to experiment with self-assessment of the quality of her processes. She had always wanted a better system of monitoring the learning process, and had begun to feel uneasy about her policy that all teachers who failed more than 20 percent of students would have a mandatory conference to explain why. Looking now at control charting, Pat wondered how many actions she had taken in the past to "fix" an entire system for problems that were actually special causes. Pat also noticed how few teachers had 20 percent failure rates the year after she announced the policy. Suddenly, it seemed as though the failure rate had made a dramatic improvement. She now realized that what was actually occurring was data manipulation. It was obvious that the teacher's reaction to this coercive quota system was not improved learning, but meeting the quota through fudging the numbers. The more she thought about it, the less she blamed them for reacting to a coercive, subjective rule via a kind of numerical prestidigitation. She then decided to keep control charts measuring the number of D's and F's that teachers gave. Statistically, this would be a fair assessment if the number of students taught by each teacher fell within a range of 25 percent of each other. The data points for the first semester are shown in the following diagram.

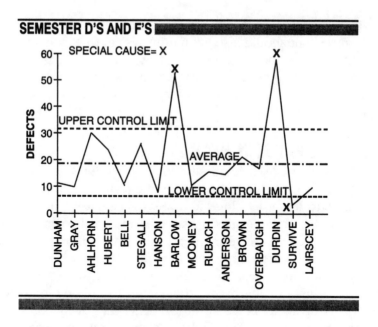

SEMESTER D'S AND F'S

SPECIAL CAUSE= X

DEFECTS

UPPER CONTROL LIMIT

AVERAGE

LOWER CONTROL LIMIT

DUNHAM GRAY AHLHORN HUBERT BELL STEGALL HANSON BARLOW MOONEY RUBACH ANDERSON BROWN OVERBAUGH DURDIN SURVIVE LAIRSCEY

The charts indicated three special causes: teachers Barlow, Durdin, and Survive. Pat was tempted to ask Mr. Ahlhorn why he had so many defects, but noticed that he was within the expected range of variation, and was therefore a common cause. She had a conference with each "special cause" teacher, opening by show-ing the data. She stated that the purpose of the conference was to discover the problem and cooperatively develop solutions. The teachers were very receptive after seeing the data and realizing that Pat was there to help. Barlow was an English as a Second Language teacher and had full enrollments in each class. She expressed frustration at not being able to make a personal impact with each student, a frustration compounded by the fact that five different languages were spoken in her classes. Pat agreed to look at reassigning an aide, and using bilingual students as peer tutors. Durdin complained that her students did not turn in their homework. After observing Durdin's classes, Pat recommended a classroom management course being taught on Saturdays. She agreed to give Durdin a substitute for one day to free her to observe several teachers on the advisory committee who were allowing students to assess their own homework for grades. When the students had ownership of the process, the rate of homework completion dramatically increased. Survive was on the CIM advisory committee and had a reputation as an explorer who tried out all the CIM points in his classes. The conference brought to light the strategies that Will was using:

1. Student survey of individual learning styles
2. Parent survey of what parents felt was important to teach
3. A joint class mission statement of what should be learned, and how it should be delivered
4. A partnership agreement with the parents on the duties of the parent and of the teacher
5. Conducting a quality circle once every two weeks, on quality in the classroom
6. Several assignments during which the students brainstorm the criteria for quality, then rate samples, and finally rate the quality of their own work
7. Allowing students to improve at home their assignments for quality
8. Cooperative learning groups
9. Lead management strategies for the achievers and role-oriented students, such as assigning achievers a leadership role in the groups and working with them on their skills, quality circles on the meaning and relevance of the lesson and unit objectives, and individual conferences to build trust and encourage success among the failure-prone students

Pat agreed to visit the class to observe this use of CIM in the classroom. She subsequently trained the steering and advisory committee members in using the statistical process control tools. The critical attribute of the training was the recognition of special and common causes. Advisory committee members were encouraged to find ways to measure and improve the learning process in the classroom. Pat knew that quality would never occur until it could be measured. She led the steering committee in examining all of the processes that have a critical impact on customer satisfaction and product service/quality. Measurement criteria from the processes were determined, and decisions were made pertaining to when the system data would be collected, where in the system data collection would occur, and who would use the data. The following table is an example of the decisions made for one process.

QUALITY ASSURANCE PLAN

PROCESS	MEASUREMENT CRITERIA	WHEN COLLECTED	INPUT, PROCESS OR OUTPUT DATA	INSTRUMENT OR TOOL	COLLECTOR OF DATA	USER
Student learning	Number of students retained	End of year	Output	Part of Performance Goal Index	Counselor	Management team

TEACHER WILL E. SURVIVE

Will was gratified that the principal had visited his class to observe students working toward quality learning. He believed the time was right to begin using SPC tools to monitor the learning in his class. He wanted to teach and involve students in quality assurance measures. His first task in teaching the statistical tools to students was to introduce the concept of *variance,* which he explained was simply *the minute differences that naturally occur in all processes.* He taught them to develop histograms and control charts, and then to distinguish between special cause and common cause. Now that the class was equipped with a set of tools, Will turned them into record keepers by requiring them to chart their grades for the next six weeks. At the end of the six weeks, the histogram for Will's class was very positively skewed. He charted the grades and discovered two special causes on the negative side. Setting the goal of paying special attention to these two students, he moved toward it by having a conference with each to determine the causes of their problems. He helped each to develop a plan for success, and assigned a peer tutor to both. The special causes dealt with family problems that Will knew would be difficult to solve, but the importance of reaching these students as far upstream as possible was all too evident. It then occurred to Will how much more clearly he saw the dynamics of student achievement since he had come to understand the concept of variation.

Once the special causes were being treated, Will knew that the responsibility for the bulk of students—now he thought of them as common causes—lay in his lap. After all, the manager manages the process, the worker works in the process. In the past he had blamed students for their lack of motivation. Now that he understood process control and common-cause reduction, he knew he had powerful tools that could make a difference in both his and his students' quests for quality. He started with a diagnostic quality circle so that he could begin breaking down the remaining barriers both among class members and between the class and himself. He structured a series of questions in the following outline:

Define questions

What was the objective of the unit/lesson?

What audiovisual aids were used?

Describe how the lesson/unit was presented.

What did you learn?

Personalize questions

How meaningful were the lesson/unit objectives?

How relevant was the content for you?

What problems did you experience with the lesson/unit?

How effective were the visual aids?

Did you enjoy the lesson/unit?

Was the evaluation a fair assessment of the learning? If not, how would you improve it?

Challenge

How would you improve the lesson/unit?

What activities would you add or delete?

How should I present the next lesson/unit?

Will discovered that the students knew and understood a lot about how one learned. The ideas he received helped to improve his instruction. He set up Quality Assurance Teams of students to monitor the classroom system. They used the quality assurance plan table to arrive at measurements they would use. One team monitored student attendance in the class by keeping a control chart of the absences and tardies. The class studied special causes and common causes to improve attendance. After reviewing the control charts, one class came up with a buddy system whereby if a person was absent he would call his assigned buddy to get the assignment.

One team kept a control chart of the number of homework assignments completed each day. From the data, Will found excessive variance in the rate of completions. He decided to allow the students to grade their own homework. Each week Will would ask each student to report verbally his or her grade for the week. Contrary to the dire warnings from his fellow teachers, Will rarely found a student who appeared to have purposely misrepresented his or her grades. Dishonesty usually would surface when the student could not make a grade on a six-weeks test comparable with the weekly averages that had been reported. A second benefit was a startling increase in the number of homework completions. It was obvious to Will that the students were taking control over their learning for the first time. He could scarcely contain the excitement, although he sensed he was annoying his fellow teachers with daily tales of breakthroughs.

Looking at the data, Will discovered that test grades and homework grades were poor indicators of learning. He found it difficult to develop tests that measured what he wanted the students to know. Tests measured content and simple skills, but concepts such as how to learn, problem-solving, and other thinking skills were hard to measure with a paper-and-pencil test. He looked for other ways for students to show they had mastered the learning. He decided to use William Glasser's New System of Concurrent Evaluation. This system had five processes. When a student was ready, he or she would show evidence of understanding the material. The teacher would ask questions, and the student would explain how what was shown was achieved. The student would then self-evaluate what was achieved, to see if it could be improved—and (if necessary) work to improve it. The evaluation and improvement process would be repeated until further attempts at improvement were judged to be not worth the effort. Glasser called this the SESIR system, for *Show, Explain, Self-evaluate, Improve, Repeat*. Will initiated the system after developing a list of competencies he felt his students should know. He kept track of the learning by using a control chart of those that were mastered. Will gave the students merit certificates when they had mastered a set number of competencies.

When Will began to use the SESIR system, he knew he would have to issue a grade at the end of the grading period. He decided only A's, B's or I's would be issued. He set a standard for quality and competence. The student would receive an A for quality and a B for competence. If the student did not reach the standard, he or she would receive an I for incomplete. The student could demonstrate competency at any time, to eliminate the I. Will longed for an abolishment of the grading system, and development of a mastery of need-to-know competencies. But—first things first, Will thought, smiling.

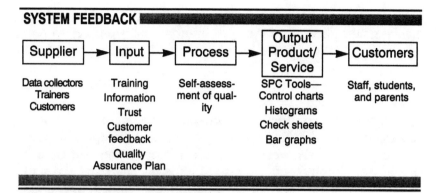

SYSTEM FEEDBACK

Supplier	→	Input	→	Process	→	Output Product/ Service	→	Customers
Data collectors Trainers Customers		Training Information Trust Customer feedback Quality Assurance Plan		Self-assessment of quality		SPC Tools— Control charts Histograms Check sheets Bar graphs		Staff, students, and parents

THE DICKINSON EXPERIENCE

In the Dickinson Independent School District a team of administrators developed a Quality Assurance Plan to ensure that the needed quality measurements would occur. Processes the district chose to monitor included:

1. Personnel hiring

2. Personnel training

3. Student learning

4. Student attendance

5. Student participation in extracurricular activities

6. Parent/community involvement in schools

7. Employee accident rates

8. Student failure/ dropout rates

9. Facility maintenance and repair quality

10. Cleanliness of facilities

11. Condition of school grounds

12. Student transportation

13. School bus condition

14. Cafeteria food service

15. Health care insurance costs

When developing a quality assurance plan it is important both to study the system and to understand the processes. In this manner the administration can monitor all parts of the system. Dickinson has eliminated the practice of evaluating people. Where the law requires a written evaluation, then a self-evaluation is used. There is no need to evaluate people. Evaluations based on rating forms or ranking methods only cause discontent and distrust. It is better to let them assess their own quality. The manager should monitor the system using SPC tools, performance goal indices, and the organization health profiles to recognize special causes. The manager should address any special cause by conferencing with the process owner(s). If the problem cannot be promptly solved, then more direct action by the manager is needed.

Instead of conducting evaluations, the manager should conference with the staff members under his/her supervision at least once every six weeks. In the conference, the participants should examine the data collected by the manager and the staff member. By examining the SPC, performance index, and organizational health data, the variance of the process can be determined and common causes reduced. This type of approach produces a team effort rather than the pitting of people against each other. When people are allowed to be responsible for the quality of their work, they will rise to meet the expectation. The few that are special causes due to worker or leader incompetence can be retrained, assigned to a job that uses their talents, or fired if there is no significant attempt to improve.

Measurement devices such as performance indices and quality assurance plans are vital tools for quality management because every organization must have a clear picture of its levels of productivity. Productivity is a measurement of the efficiency of the system—a comparison between the amount of inputs placed in the system and the amount of outputs. Those inputs that do not add value to the outputs are waste. Efficiency/productivity also involves the time to move the inputs through the process and on to outputs. Any time spent that does not add value to the outputs is waste. It is management's responsibility to manage in a way that makes the system more efficient, and thus more productive. Effectiveness is that improvement of the process which eliminates defects and increases the satisfaction of the customer. Effectiveness is related to quality. In monitoring a system, management must consider effectiveness/productivity and effectiveness/quality criteria.

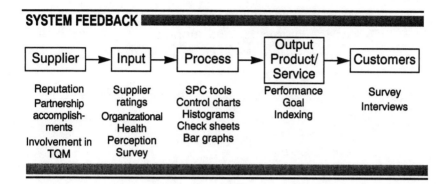

Supplier	Input	Process	Output Product/ Service	Customers
Reputation Partnership accomplish- ments Involvement in TQM	Supplier ratings Organizational Health Perception Survey	SPC tools Control charts Histograms Check sheets Bar graphs	Performance Goal Indexing	Survey Interviews

MANAGEMENT PRINCIPLES USED

ORGANIZING

Delivering information to process owners and organizing who will monitor which processes:

1. Who will collect data
2. When data will be collected
3. Where data will be collected
4. How data will be delivered to user

PLANNING

1. Develop Quality Assurance Plan for monitoring the system.
2. Ensure that all components of the system are measured for continuous improvement.

CONTROLLING

Understanding and using principles in the third correlate: Assess Own Quality

1. Understand process variation and use SPC tools for measuring defects.
2. Eliminate performance evaluations and merit pay based on performance.
3. Measure input of suppliers for quality.
4. Reduce reliance on grades as indicator of student mastery of learning.
5. Allow all workers to assess and improve their own processes:

    a. Delegate authority.

    b. Provide information and support.

    c. Develop trust in the organization.

    d. Train workers in SPC Tools.

6. Management should organize and plan for monitoring the system:

    a. Check sheets

    b. Control charts

    c. Histograms

    d. Performance indexes

    e. OHI

    f. Survey information

7. Promote Strategic or System planning.

LEADING

Building trust, developing a risk-free environment, and eliminating barriers to self-assessment.

CHAPTER 6

Focus on Quality Opportunities

Continuous Improvement schools use systematic management techniques to identify and understand defects and waste, and to forge a consensus on ways to reduce those defects. These techniques, referred to collectively as Quality Process Control (QPC), are used as tools, in much the same way that a plumber uses a wrench to fix pipes, or a carpenter uses a saw to cut wood. Tools make work easier by improving the productivity of labor. QPC tools make the task of defining and implementing quality easier by offering standard approaches to tackling problems. Perhaps problems is an incorrect label for the challenges faced by managers who strive for quality; maybe opportunities is a better word. At any rate, to identify and reduce quality opportunities, empowered workers not only must have effective tools, but also must be trained in their use.

CIM organizations identify, analyze, and solve quality problems and opportunities with the following QPC tools, which have been grouped into three categories: Information-gathering tools, consensus-development tools, and problem-identification and process-analysis tools.

INFORMATION-GATHERING TOOLS

TOOL NUMBER 1: BRAINSTORMING

Brainstorming, most recently and fully developed by advertising executive Alex Osborne in the 1950s, is a simple, enjoyable technique used to tap the creative talents of group members. It generates a large number of ideas—even some that seem silly or ridiculous. Brainstorming can be used in many aspects of the problem-solving process, such as identifying, analyzing, and presenting alternative solutions. Brainstorming is a powerful tool because it effectively utilizes an entire group's thinking resources, rather than those of one individual with limited knowledge. While there are numerous variations on the brainstorming theme, two are the most commonly used in industry: Open brainstorming, which is done out loud in a group, and Nominal Group Process Technique, which is performed individually, with the results shared by the group.

Open Brainstorming

1. Members must first understand and adhere to certain brainstorming rules. These are:

   a. All ideas are to be stated, no matter how inconsequential they seem. Quantity, not quality, is sought.

   b. No criticism of ideas is allowed. If members' ideas are attacked, they will feel self-conscious and will not fully participate.

   c. Building on others' ideas (piggybacking) is desirable.

   d. Everyone is encouraged to participate, whether in an open forum or round-robin.

   e. Adequate time must be devoted to the session.

2. All members must understand the issue to be addressed. A clear problem definition is essential.

3. One member serves as recorder, listing on paper mounted on an easel in clear view of all group members all ideas that are generated.

4. When the session ends, members review all ideas, selecting the appropriate ones for further consideration.

Nominal Group Process Technique

Nominal Group Process brainstorming has the same objective as the method just described, but a slightly different procedure. NGP starts out as a silent approach instead of a vocal one during the idea stages. This approach may be more appropriate than group brainstorming when group members feel uncomfortable with each other, or with the process of brainstorming itself. Once the ideas are written and collected, however, discussion follows.

How to Conduct an NGP Brainstorming Session

1. **Problem statement:** Post a clear statement of the problem on a flip chart or blackboard within easy sight of all group members.

2. **Silent generation of ideas:** Without group discussion, ask each participant to spend about 10 minutes writing ideas in response to the problem statement.

3. **Round-robin:** Begin by setting an approximate time limit for the session. Fifteen minutes is usually a good length, but continue if the group is still involved. Each participant contributes one idea at a time in round-robin fashion while a group recorder lists each idea on a flip chart or sheets of newsprint. After a few trips around the circle, participants should feel free to suggest their ideas without regard to whose turn it is.

4. **Clarification:** Discuss each idea from the list in turn to clarify meaning, eliminate duplications, and allow group members to express general agreement or disagreement with an item. Try to look for combinations of ideas and areas of agreement. Record on the flip chart all changes to the original list.

Brainstorming is used to gather ideas in a short amount of time. To further clarify the ideas generated by brainstorming, an excellent tool is "The Six Thinking Hats."

TOOL NUMBER 2: THE SIX THINKING HATS

Edward DeBono, an expert in the field of creative problem-solving, refined the concept of role-playing with a strategy he introduced in the book *The Six Thinking Hats*. Recognizing that the greatest enemy of thinking is complexity, which in turn leads to confusion, he proposed the notion of the Six Thinking Hats with two purposes in mind:

1. Simplify thinking by allowing a participant to deal with one strain of thought at a time, instead of juggling the systems of emotions, logic, information, hope, and creativity all at once.

2. Allow thinkers to make a switch in their thinking, so that they don't get stuck in a particular (usually the negative) mode.

DeBono compares the Six Thinking Hats to the process of printing a color map. Each color is printed separately, but all layers must come together synchronously in order to make sense of the map. DeBono believes that creativity is enhanced when thinkers begin to break down their statements in the same way in which a color map's stratified layers can be separated. During the process of changing hats, the discussion becomes brisk and disciplined, rather than drifting and declining in value. The discussion leader uses the six hats by recalling the essence of each hat, and recording input on each and then moving on to the next one. DeBono describes the six hats as:

Red Hat (seeing red; emotions and feelings; also hunch and intuition; legitimizing emotions and feelings so that they can become part of the "thinking map"): There should never be an attempt to justify feelings, or provide a logical basis for them.

White Hat (virgin white; pure facts; figures and information; neutrality): Imitate a computer and ask focused questions in order to obtain information or identify information gaps.

Black Hat (devil's advocate; obstacles; why it will not work; pointing out how something does not fit experience or accepted knowledge; noting faults in design): It is not argument and should not be seen as such, nor is it an excuse to cover negative indulgence or feelings (which should make use of the red hat).

Yellow Hat (sunshine, brightness and optimism; constructive; opportunity; concerned with positive assessment): It probes for value and benefit, seeking to make things happen.

Green Hat (fertile; creative; plants spring from seeds; movement; provocation; recognizing the need to go beyond the known, the obvious, and the satisfactory): The green-hat thinker is concerned more with moving along rather than with judging.

Blue Hat (cool and controlled; orchestra conductor; thinking about thinking): The blue-hat thinker defines the subject and sets the focus, defining the problems and shaping the thinking. It ensures that the rules of the game are observed. While this role may be assigned to a particular individual, anyone can wear this hat at any time.

Using the Six Hats

When discussing an issue, identifying a problem, or deciding on causes, the Six Hats tool will help clarify all aspects of the subject. The group leader usually will begin by asking for comments on the subject while symbolically "wearing" the red hat. Since most issues hit an emotional nerve in at least one group member, it is best to get those feelings out at the start. The group leader likely will move next to the white hat, balancing emotions with research-based data, findings from actual tests, data from SPC tools, performance goal indices, organizational health profiles, surveys, and other measurement data. Just the facts, not opinions. The yellow hat should follow so that the group can turn its attention to positives, strengths, and ideals. Moving to the green hat next gives the group a chance to get "out of the box" and brainstorm alternatives to its established course of thinking. The black hat should follow in order to examine weaknesses in the alternatives. Last, the blue hat organizes the ideas into categories, problems, or rankings.

TOOL NUMBER 3: SURVEYS OR QUESTIONNAIRES

Surveys and questionnaires are excellent methods for obtaining information from customers or suppliers, both external and internal. Rather than survey all customers and suppliers, it is best to sample the population. A random selection of 10 percent of the population would provide statistically accurate data. A common survey format asks questions that call for the respondent to choose from a variety of levels of agreement or disagreement. This range might be stated by the terms strongly agree, agree, no opinion, disagree, and strongly disagree. Schools can design surveys on preprinted forms, to enable the respondent to shade in answers that can be computer-read. This greatly simplifies the labor required to collate survey results.

The steps in designing a questionnaire are:
1. Identify the data you want to obtain.
2. Determine the universe of respondents.
3. Devise a system for sampling the universe of respondents.
4. Design the questionnaire.
5. Pretest it with a small group.
6. Gain approval to conduct it.

TOOL NUMBER 4: BENCHMARKING

It is a natural human tendency to compare everything we do with the standard of quality in our endeavors. Before implementing a new program, we typically shop around to see how the "best of the best" do it. This has informally been called *benchmarking,* and schools have commonly benchmarked by word of mouth, visits to other schools, or gathering information at conferences. As a QPC tool, benchmarking is a structured method of gathering data to be used to reach solutions. Once the criterion for a solution is established, the search should begin for an example of the desired criterion that meets world-class standards—or at least state-class standards.

The steps to using benchmarking are:

1. Identify what is to be benchmarked.
2. Identify comparative organizations.
3. Determine the data to be collected.
4. Determine the current performance "gap."
5. Project future performance levels.
6. Communicate benchmark findings, and gain acceptance thereof.
7. Establish functional goals.
8. Develop action plans.
9. Implement specific actions, and monitor progress.

The benefits of benchmarking are:

1. Improved ability to meet customer requirements.
2. Assurance that organization goals reflect external realities.
3. Improved measurements of productivity.
4. Enhanced competitive position.
5. Greater awareness of the industry's best practices.

CONSENSUS-DEVELOPMENT TOOLS

TOOL NUMBER 5: TEN–FOUR CONSENSUS VOTING

Ten–Four voting is a method for arriving at consensus through rounds of voting. Once the list of items to be voted on has been brainstormed, each member gets ten total votes. For each round of voting, each member can cast between zero and four votes, unless of course he or she has less than four votes left to cast. Every member can allocate the votes any way he or she sees fit. For example, a group member may cast all four votes for one item in round one, two for one item and two for another in the second round, and the remaining two for another item in the third, for a total of ten votes.

Group members may pass on a round of voting. If they do, they can vote at the end of the rotation or wait until the next round. The rounds continue until each member has cast ten votes. The votes are then tallied, and the list is ranked by the total of votes for each item.

Consensus voting allows each member to have a voice in the process of deciding what the group thinks, but it has an additional benefit. As the voting progresses, the team members see the votes of their peers, and often begin to rethink their preferences. Such action usually assists in developing consensus. Whether or not that occurs, Ten–Four voting is a reliable measurement of the degree of agreement that group members have for the items on which they are voting.

TOOL NUMBER 6: 5–3–1 CONSENSUS RATINGS

In this consensus-forming technique, each team member should rate each item using a five for very important, three for somewhat important, and one for of very little importance. The members should agree on which percent of the maximum ratings an item could receive will constitute consensus. For example, if there were six members of the team, each item could receive a maximum rating of thirty. If the members agreed on 80 percent as consensus, then any item receiving twenty-four rating points would be considered for study (.80 × 30 = 24).

TOOL NUMBER 7: PARETO DIAGRAMS

"Twenty percent of the people own eighty percent of the nation's wealth" is an example of the Pareto Principle, this attributed to Vilfredo Pareto, an Italian economist who observed the maldistribution of incomes in his society. In short, Pareto observed that a few persons have big incomes and many have small incomes. An American quality-control specialist, Dr. Joseph M. Juran, adapted Pareto's concept to the incidence of defects in industrial manufacture. For the purposes of productivity, the Pareto Principle may be stated as "80 percent of the defects come from 20 percent of the sources." Also called The Law of the Vital Few and the Trivial Many, or The 80/20 Rule, the Pareto Principle is frequently applied to a variety of personal and organizational management issues—time utilization, staff conflicts, equipment and communication breakdowns, and the like. Educators observe the Pareto Principle in their schools when they see that 80 percent of the absences are caused by 20 percent of the students, 80 percent of the staff complaints come from 20 percent of the faculty, and 80 percent of parent volunteer work is done by 20 percent of the parents (ask any PTA volunteer to validate Pareto).

Problem-solvers use Pareto diagrams to identify and select those problems which, if solved, would have a major impact on improving the quality and productivity of the process. Furthermore, the crucial task of winnowing the vital few problems from the trivial chaff is made easier by applying the Pareto principle to develop a Pareto diagram according to the following steps:

1. Collect information on all of the reasons or precipitating factors that might cause the selected problem to occur. Record data on how often these potential factors occur and the resultant time, financial cost, or frequency connected with each. A check sheet may be used to collect and present the information.

2. Construct a table displaying the factors from greatest to smallest according to frequency, dollar cost, lost time, or whatever standard is appropriate. Combine the very minor problems into one group labeled "other." This group is always last even if it is not the smallest.

3. Calculate the percentage for each problem by using the formula: Frequency divided by total = percent of total.

4. Determine the cumulative percent by starting with the percent of total for the first problem. List that percentage, then add to it the percentage for the second problem. For example, if the first problem is 32 percent of the total and the second problem is 22 percent of the total, the cumulative percent of the two would be 54 percent. Continue to add each percentage to the previous total until you reach 100 percent.

5. Using this information, you are now ready to construct the Pareto diagram.

Problem	Frequency	% of Total	Cumulative %
Bus breakdowns	25	31	31
Late arrivals	20	25	56
Driver unavailability	15	19	75
Other	20	25	100
Total	80	100	N.A.

The steps in constructing a pareto diagram are:

1. Draw the horizontal and vertical axes for the diagram. Divide the space on the horizontal axis to evenly display the entire number of problems you identified (four in our example).

2. On the left-hand vertical axis, construct a scale with the total frequency at the top, descending to zero at the bottom.

3. On the right-hand vertical axis, construct a scale depicting the percentages, with the 100 percent maximum directly across from the corresponding total frequency.

4. Construct a column graph using information from your table. Place the first item on your chart in the first space and draw the column at the appropriate height. Repeat this process for each problem.

5. To plot the cumulative line, place a dot in line with the top right corner of each column. That dot should be at a height corresponding to the number in the cumulative percentage column of your work sheet.

6. Connect the dots, beginning with the lower left corner of the diagram.

7. Label the axes, and add a legend showing the source of data, dates, areas where it was collected, who collected it, and any other pertinent data.

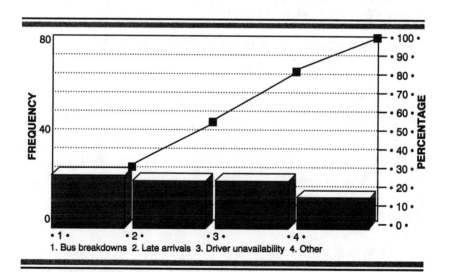

1. Bus breakdowns 2. Late arrivals 3. Driver unavailability 4. Other

TOOL NUMBER 8: THE DELPHI TECHNIQUE

Another ranking and reducing tool is the Delphi Technique. From a list of brainstormed ideas, group members individually rank their preferences in declining vote order. The number of votes for the top preference is one-half the total number of ideas. For example, if there are twenty items, then a member's first choice will receive ten votes, the second choice will receive nine votes, and so on, until the last choice receives one vote. Half of the brainstormed ideas will not receive any of the individual member's votes. After each member votes, a group leader totals the votes and places them in rank order by preference. Only the top sixteen (80 percent of the original list) are placed on the next ballot. Members then vote on this new list, using the same principle. The member's first choice receives eight votes (one-half of sixteen). This will reduce the list to twelve or thirteen. You may continue this technique as many times as you want to reduce the list. Long lists may require several voting rounds to get the list to a workable number. It is important to list the votes each time the list is given to the members, so they can see how others rated the choices.

Another way to get consensus is by using the Delphi Technique repeatedly until the order does not change. After each ranking, the items not getting votes will be eliminated.

PROBLEM IDENTIFICATION AND PROCESS ANALYSIS TOOLS

TOOL NUMBER 9: PROCESS FLOW DIAGRAMS

Since understanding a process is the first step to improving it, groups using CIM need a visual tool to diagram their processes. One such is a process flow diagram (PFD). Often called a *flow chart,* a process flow diagram is a pictorial explanation of the activities in any process, from the very beginning of that process to the end-point. It has many benefits, the greatest being its usefulness in identifying all the customers of a given process. Process flow diagrams also provide an understanding of the entire process, which helps to provide missing pieces of the picture. Other benefits include identifying opportunities for improvement by pinpointing duplicative effort or *loops.*

Process flow diagrams help explain both organizational and personal situations. For example, someone can use a flow chart to understand personal situations such as a chronically over-drawn bank account, or tardiness to important meetings. In a business example, we may use a process flow diagram to study how invoices are processed, how new employees learn their jobs, etc. In schools, flow charts can be used to diagram how students learn to read, or play an instrument, and how staff members select which facts to present to students—and so on.

How to Draw a Process Flow Diagram

1. Decide on the process to study.
2. Write down the steps that appear to be part of the process. Remember, you are diagraming how things actually work, not how you believe they should work. Don't be concerned with the order of the steps—just get them on paper.
3. Prioritize the steps chronologically by putting "1" by the first step, etc.
4. Sketch out the step-by-step process, using the symbols shown below, in the "Legends" section. (A very large process may require several smaller PFD's.)
5. Review your drawing with others who are involved in the process to ensure that your diagram is complete. (You may be amazed at the feedback you get, and the additions to your diagram).
6. Apply problem-solving techniques (such as brainstorming), role-playing, and other methods to locate the places where problems arise. This will help you to focus your team's efforts to improve the process.

Legends

Since PFD's are visual representations, they use symbols to denote activities. The following diagram shows you which symbol stands for which step.

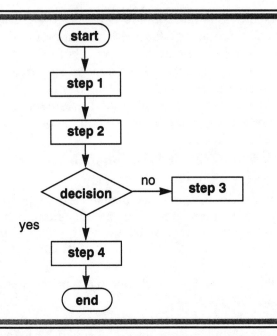

TOOL NUMBER 10: CAUSE-AND-EFFECT DIAGRAMS

While brainstorming generates ideas on possible causes of defects, the cause-and-effect diagram accomplishes much the same purpose in a more structured format. It helps members to evaluate complex problems involving many variable causes by assisting them in identifying and sorting all the possible causes of a problem and then displaying them on one sheet of paper so that all aspects may be easily seen and considered.

A commonly used cause-and-effect diagram is the *random-method fishbone diagram.* It is called a fishbone diagram because, when completed, it resembles the skeletal outlines of a fish. It is "random" because causes are suggested in no specific order for any category of the diagram.

Steps in Creating a Fishbone Diagram

1. Identify the problem the group has chosen to work on. This is the "effect," so it is placed in the "effect" box on the right margin of the diagram. Examples of "effects" would be slow response time for customer complaints, high student retention rate, or low student participation in after-school tutoring.

2. Draw a long arrow leading to the effect, representing those things that contribute to the effect.

3. Decide what the major categories of causes of the effect are, and list them on branches of the arrow. Four commonly used categories are equipment, materials, procedures, and people. These can be changed for different problems.

4. Members suggest specific causes, which are placed under the major category to which they pertain. Brainstorming is used to generate ideas. The facilitator should ask "Why?" after each reason for the effect is suggested. This technique is used by the Japanese, who ask "Why?" five times for each cause that is brainstormed. The responses should be written down as branches under the original cause.

5. Causes may be modified. This type of addition is positioned by connecting it with a branch to the original cause listed.

6. The diagram should be posted for several days in a highly visible place, for all members to review and add to.

7. Members begin eliminating the trivial or less significant causes by drawing lines through them.

8. Members discuss the remaining causes and group them together if they agree that two or more are similar.

9. The remaining causes can be numbered for ease of reference, and used for Ten–Four Consensus Voting, to arrive at a Pareto diagram on causes.

It is important to save the completed diagram. Members may use it at their presentation to demonstrate that all causes were considered, thus adding validity to the solution being proposed.

CAUSE-AND-EFFECT DIAGRAM

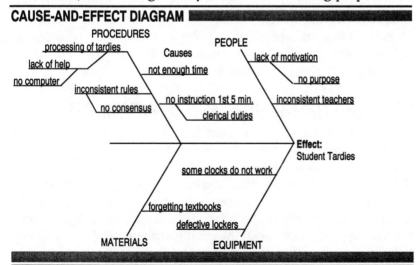

Identifying Quality Opportunities

The above tools help organizations to arrive at the causes of problems by assisting them in collecting and using data. These tools sharpen the focus on potential solutions, and often cause scales to fall from the eyes of those who have been blinded from reality by fuzzy subjectivity or lack of hard data. For example, a group studying the problem of student tardiness may find, after using the information-gathering tools, that increases in student tardiness are directly related to the arrival time of school buses, and not to factors over which students have control. The group's understanding of bus arrivals would be enhanced by using the problem-identification tools of process flow diagrams and fishbone diagrams. By using the consensus tools of Ten–Four Voting and Pareto diagrams, the group can come to agreement on the sources of the problem.

When focusing on quality opportunities to study, it is vitally important to begin with data. By analyzing accurate data, defects and waste will become apparent. Control charts of processes will help determine special and common causes to study. Histograms of processes will indicate possible problems with the process. Surveys of customers will show levels of satisfaction and dissatisfaction. Performance goal indexes will indicate discrepancies in products and services, discrepancies that should be traced back to processes for the spotting of problems. Organizational health profiles will show strengths and weaknesses in group working relationships. By using all of these methods, a group can begin with data and facts. When staff members bring their problems to a group's or leader's attention, they should be asked for data to validate the problems. Educators are known for chasing rabbits, only to catch gophers. Thus, we often attempt to solve problems that are not problems at all. The data should indicate if there are defects or waste, or at least give significant clues for further investigation.

FOCUSING ON THE VITAL FEW OPPORTUNITIES

Common causes are the responsibility of management. Most waste and defects are the result of common causes. To attempt to reduce all common causes in the system would sap the energy of the managers. (Recall that Pareto says that remedying 20 percent of all causes would solve 80 percent of our problems.) Managers do not have the time needed to solve all of the problems that fall into their baskets, although most American managers today act as if they believe they can. All organizations striving for quality must have a prioritizing process in order to work on only the vital few problems at any given time. A fishbone can help trace the vital few.

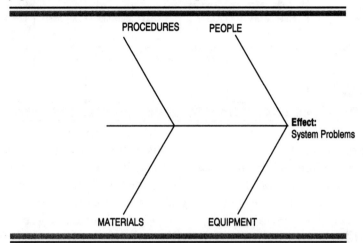

PROCEDURES   PEOPLE

Effect:
System Problems

MATERIALS   EQUIPMENT

Again, problems can be clarified by asking "Why?" many times. In this manner the core problem can be distinguished from symptoms and vague issues. After completion of the cause-effect diagram, the core problems should be grouped under main topics or headings, with similar problems fused into one. The problems are then lettered for ease in both discussion and consensus-gathering. Now is also the time to restate the problem as a project statement. The essential elements of a project statement are:

1. **Direction of Change**—increase or decrease
2. **Measure of Quality**—number of and cost of
3. **Relationship to a Process**—bus driving, learning, preparing food, repairing vehicles, coaching, teaching, maintaining equipment, typing reports, producing payroll, balancing ledgers, etc.

Example: To decrease the amount of time to process purchase orders.

The Six Hats tool should be used with each quality opportunity (project statement). This tool will help identify key components of the problem. After using the Six Hats, analyze the system for each problem. A matrix for accomplishing this objective is displayed on page 90.

The project statement is "To decrease the number of discipline cases in managing student behavior." The value to the customer is high, and the time frame for the solution is this school year. The trend of the problem is to worsen if nothing is done. If the problem had high value to the customer and was an emergency, then it would probably receive a high ranking as a problem for focus.

Project Statement	Authority for Final Decision	Process Owners	Process	Customers	Suppliers	High- Medium- Low-Value to Customer
To decrease the number of discipline cases in managing student behavior	Management team	Teachers Assistant principal	Managing student behavior	Students Teachers Parents	Parents Consultants	High

Next, a consensus tool should be used in order to get agreement. The Ten–Four Consensus Voting is ideal in a retreat setting where all the tools can be used in one period of time. A Pareto Diagram of the votes should be used to determine the vital few. As seen by examining the graph, the vital few become the problems receiving 80 percent of the votes. The remaining problems are the trivial many. The time for solving the trivial many may be in the future, but the energy of the organization needs to focus now on the vital few.

CHARTERING TEAMS

Now that the vital few have been identified, the committee or team responsible for developing them must determine the type of team to charter for solving the problem. There are five types of teams that can be chartered. One is a Customer/Supplier Team. If the problem has clearly identified internal customers and suppliers who share in the conundrum, then a customer/supplier team might help open communication and break down barriers between the groups. If there is recognition that these groups can work out the problem, then a charter is in order. Customer/supplier teams usually deal with cross-functional problems, meaning that two or more process owners are involved, with one a supplier to the other.

The second type is a Process Improvement Team. If the problem has a clear process with distinct process owners, then it is a candidate for a process improvement team composed of process owners and (possibly) customers of the process. If the process is difficult to ascertain, or is ill-defined, then these are clues that there may be a need to restructure a process, or design a new one. A Design/Redesign Team is then needed. The fourth type is a Study Team. A study team's purpose is to investigate an issue, to see if in fact there is a problem. When the purpose or problem is not clear, then a study team is in order. Study teams are also used to evaluate a program or implementation strategy.

The fifth type of team is an Implementation Team. An implementation team's function is to put into action recommendations or strategies developed by others. This team's responsibility is to institutionalize the change by acting on the system.

Once the the problem has been identified, the system for the problem analyzed, and the type of team designated, a charter needs to be developed. The type of team designated to study the problem determines the content of the charter. The charter needs to spell out the purpose of the team, the scope of the team's authority, the members of the team, and who will facilitate, chair, and sponsor the team. The purpose of problem-solving teams is to attain a breakthrough. A breakthrough is a planned change in the process that reduces the defects or waste in the system. (Problem-solving teams often are called breakthrough teams.) The purpose should spell out the reasons for the team's being chartered, a statement of the problem, and the data used by the parent team or committee to identify and clarify the problem.

Since the scope of the team is its parameters, it is important to state what limits the team has to its recommendations. If costs or additional personnel are a factor, then state the team's scope in these areas. If the parent team has a time limit, that should be stated in the scope. The parent team must accept the chartered team's recommendation 99 percent of the time, if the team has used the tools properly to reduce the effects of the problem. The parent team can send the recommendation back for study, but must guard against making changes. Chartered teams will not pursue their purpose diligently if there is the threat that the recommendation will not be accepted and acted on. The scope is precisely where the parent team can set limits which will help deliver a recommended change that will be acceptable.

The members of the team should be picked with careful attention to their concern for the problem. People with little concern for the problem to be studied will probably not work to solve it. A *chairperson* should be designated to develop the agenda; set a time, date, and place for gathering; and conduct the meeting. The team must have a facilitator trained in the use of QPC tools and how to build teamwork. *This is the most important role on the team.* The success of the team depends on both the use of the tools and team-building skills. Another important role is the team sponsor, a member of the parent team whose role is to make sure the team is successful. The sponsor needs to open doors for the team, provide needed resources, and report back to the parent team the progress of the chartered team. There are other roles for team members, but they should be left to the team to designate. These roles could be *timekeeper, recorder, consensus checker, data collector,* and *caretaker*—a person responsible for the comfort and physical well-being of the team.

REALITY THERAPY CONFERENCING

Not all quality opportunities are common causes that can be solved by teams. There are special causes that often prevent common causes from being studied. It is the job of lead managers to eliminate special causes before tackling the common-cause opportunities. The process cannot get in control without elimination of the special causes, which are controlled by the worker in the process. Most of the time, extraordinary circumstances create the special cause. If the special cause is attributed to worker error, managers should have a conference with the worker, using the principles of Reality Therapy.

Reality therapy is an effective counseling tool for lead managers to use with special-cause behavior or problems. William Glasser developed reality therapy as a method of helping people to examine and evaluate their behaviors, and develop plans for improvement. It is based on Glasser's concept of Control Theory, which explains why humans behave as they do, and why fear and coercion never produce quality. Understanding control theory is crucial to understanding why reality therapy works. (An explanation of the theory is found in Chapter 4.)

To capsulize: Each person behaves to meet one or more of five needs—power, fun, freedom, love, and survival. These needs are fundamental to our being (Glasser says they are built into our DNA), and we can choose only those behaviors that will best satisfy these needs. Fear and coercion do not satisfy these needs. While it is possible to get some productive work from these methods, *no one* will do quality work over the long term under pressure from coercion and fear; consistent work experiences of these insidious forces shut down the brain's ability to use the creative powers that so often define quality. Under a system ruled by fear, employees invariably choose the safest course of action—which rarely is the most creative one.

Given these circumstances, a counselor or friend can recognize when we are trapped in a cycle of choosing ineffective behaviors. A counselor using reality therapy can help us to choose behaviors that will help satisfy our wants. Control theory teaches that we have a total behavioral system that consists of *feelings, physical well-being, thinking,* and *doing.* Our behaviors are always a mixture of actions, thoughts, and physical states, deeply intertwined so that a change in one area causes changes in the others. The goal of the reality therapist is to help the client choose a "doing" behavior, knowing that if it works, the person will experience more positive thoughts, feel better and become less stressed. Feelings, thoughts, and physical well-being are difficult to change for the better when the focus is on them. Trying to feel better without doing something that satisfies our needs is very difficult. We can train ourselves to think positive thoughts in an attempt to produce positive actions. However, it is easier to concentrate on the "doing" rather than the "thinking" to produce positive thoughts. Using reality therapy can help out-of-control people to learn to manage their lives. Teachers, students, parents, and managers all should learn both control theory and reality therapy, in order to understand why humans behave as they do, as well as how they can work with each other to choose mutually satisfying, quality-producing behaviors.

Reality therapy nevertheless does not work in the absence of trust. Lead managers cannot eliminate special causes without building trust with the workers. This trust can be developed through private conferences with workers, and by showing courtesy even when the worker does not respond in kind. Lead managers refrain from criticism because it destroys trust. They use constructive feedback instead to focus on facts rather than opinions, and the future rather than the past. The four steps of reality therapy are shown in the chart on page 94.

Reality therapy is by far the most effective approach to quality improvement. When a person is out of control, the following four steps can be used in conferencing or counseling.

Step 1: Evaluate/Focus

Lead managers begin by focusing on what need/want the person is trying to satisfy. They ask him or her to evaluate how successfully his or her behavior is satisfying that need/want. Four questions lead managers may ask are: (1) What are/were you doing? (2) Did it work? Or is it working? (3) What do you want to happen? (4) What could you do to get that to happen?

People do not change irresponsible behavior unless they understand that it is not satisfying their needs/wants, or the needs/wants of friends. Lead managers get workers/students to focus on their behavior and to self-evaluate the results thereof.

Because there is trust, it is understood that the manager wants to help, not punish. In this climate of trust, it is easy to show that their behavior is not only hurting them, but also both their friends and the quality of their work.

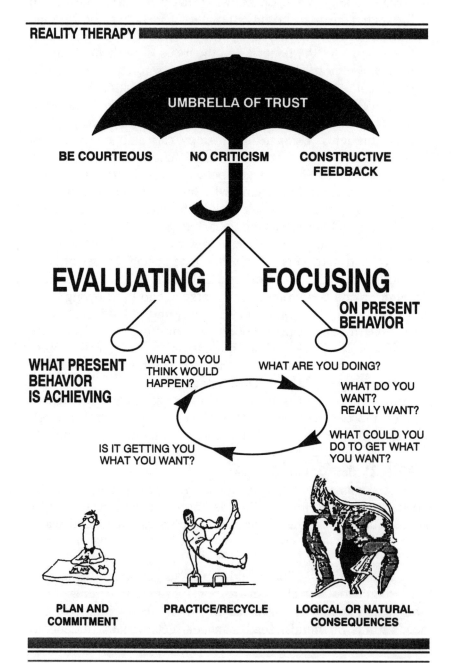

REALITY THERAPY

UMBRELLA OF TRUST

BE COURTEOUS   NO CRITICISM   CONSTRUCTIVE FEEDBACK

EVALUATING   **FOCUSING**

ON PRESENT BEHAVIOR

WHAT PRESENT BEHAVIOR IS ACHIEVING

WHAT DO YOU THINK WOULD HAPPEN?

WHAT ARE YOU DOING?

WHAT DO YOU WANT? REALLY WANT?

WHAT COULD YOU DO TO GET WHAT YOU WANT?

IS IT GETTING YOU WHAT YOU WANT?

PLAN AND COMMITMENT   PRACTICE/RECYCLE   LOGICAL OR NATURAL CONSEQUENCES

Step 2: Plan/Commitment

Once the person recognizes that it is his or her choice of behaviors that is causing problems, the conference should move to the planning stage. The plan is simply to discover which behavior the person would be willing to follow in order to improve the situation. The commitment is what the person will do immediately. The manager should determine whether he or she will commit to a trial period for a day or week. It is important to remember that *everyone's* behavior occurs in order to satisfy quality wants. When out of control, we sometimes try bizarre behavior to get back into control. Obviously we believe this will work, or we would not try it. Students try a lot of "dumb" behavior in an attempt to get friends (belongings), attention (recognition), fun, and freedom into their lives. It is our task to substitute more productive behaviors that will eventually satisfy these needs and wants.

Step 3: Practice/Recycle

Practicing new behaviors means taking a risk. People take risks only for people they trust. As we have seen, reality therapy will not work if there is no trust. During the trial period the new behavior *must* work, or else the person may return to the irresponsible behaviors. Irresponsible behaviors get attention and can be freedom-producing, so it is crucial for the person to gain recognition, belonging, more choices, and pleasure from the "new and improved" behaviors. A lead manager will provide most of these needs during the practice period. Once the new behaviors become comfortable, they will provide the satisfaction needed, with only occasional involvement by the manager.

If the person reverts to old, unproductive behaviors, then it is time to start over. How many times the lead manager recycles in the attempt to change behavior depends on the degree of irresponsible behavior, how long the person in question has practiced it, and the support of the home environment.

Step 4: Logical/Natural Consequences

Lead managers do not protect people from their own irresponsible behaviors. A person must experience logical consequences developed and agreed on by the organization, department, team, or class. Many times, parents want to protect their children from the natural results of the kids' behavior. This is counterproductive, however, since behavior changes only when a person sees that his or her behavior is not working (not helping to achieve the basic needs). Allowing logical consequences to occur is not punishment, because the choice toward behavioral change rests with the individual and not the lead manager. Once a plan is developed and agreed on, then it is a new day. Starting fresh is the key. Lead managers do not give up on workers.

PRINCIPAL PAT ANN HOLD

Trail's End Middle School had become a kinder and gentler place since the staff was introduced to the principles of CIM. Pat's efforts to become a lead manager seemed to be reaping dividends in increasing openness and trust. A significant number of teachers were willing to rethink everything they were doing with kids, or (as they now said), everything they had been doing to kids. However, the new atmosphere also gave off the scent of confusion, as staff members wondered what would come after the introduction of the new philosophy. Everyone seemed to sense that the change to CIM would involve significant and potentially unsettling change, but no one seemed to know what that change would look like.

While Managing While Wandering Around, Pat sensed the uncertainty. She knew the next step was to begin solving problems by using a team approach that utilized the tools everyone was learning. "That's the only way we can demonstrate by our actions what we want everyone to begin doing," she thought. Pat shared her feelings with the steering committee, who also expressed the sentiment that the time was ripe for problem-solving, using the new techniques. The committee decided to use the tools to focus on problems they felt confident in tackling and which offered the greatest chance for early, demonstrable success. This last point is critical: The first problem selected by a team should be one in which the team stands a high degree of achieving success. It should also be a problem that has a high profile with the staff. The benefits of solving the problem should have benefits for all or most of the staff.

The committee began by studying the existing data from their quality assurance plan measurements, to get an overview of the major problem areas at Trail's End. It wasn't a pretty picture: The organizational health inventory indicated that staff cohesiveness was low. The performance goal index showed that the students from low socioeconomic families were learning at an inferior rate. The few control charts that were kept by the principal depicted a problem with student attendance and discipline. A survey of the parents showed a lack of parent involvement, and the teacher survey concurred with this perception. Too, the analysis of supplier input indicated that students were entering the school without prerequisite skills for success.

Further problems surfaced as the committee analyzed the data. When opinions were expressed, the facilitator asked for facts. The committee soon felt overwhelmed with the problems that had faced Pat. One member suggested picking a problem area to solve by blindfold. Amid the halfhearted chuckles, a member asked if Pat could arrange for the committee to visit a school she had benchmarked for their involvement with CIM. This gave the committee a renewed faith that the quality approach would work to solve problems and reduce defects and waste.

The benchmarking visit to Quality Land Middle School opened the committee members' eyes. They saw a school with the same socioeconomic characteristics as Trail's End, but with a greater degree of student success and staff cohesiveness. Quality Land was five years into its CIM journey. Returning home, the steering committee regained its commitment to using the tools, to plunge into identifying quality opportunities to solve. It first used a cause-and-effect diagram to brainstorm various quality opportunities. DeBono's Six Hats were used to gain a better understanding of the problems. Ten–Four Voting followed, to get consensus. And the accompanying Pareto diagram revealed the vital few problems, as indicated in the committee's vote totals.

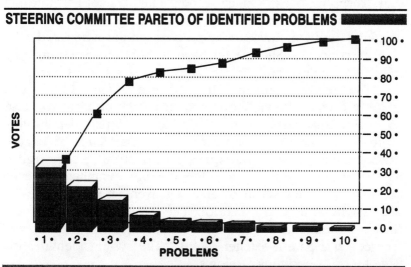

STEERING COMMITTEE PARETO OF IDENTIFIED PROBLEMS

Problems:

1. Management of student behavior
2. Discrepancy between success of low socioeconomic students and others
3. Lack of parent involvement
4. Cohesiveness of the staff
5. Late arrival of buses
6. Lunchroom behavior of students
7. Schedule of classes
8. Excessive tardies
9. Food in the cafeteria
10. Lack of time for planning

The top 80 percent of problems, the vital few, were the first four problems: management of student behavior, discrepancy between success of low socioeconomic students and others, lack of parent involvement, and low cohesiveness of the staff. The remaining problems, the trivial many that plague staff members, were put on the shelf for study at a later time. In fact, Pat believed that resolving the vital few would probably solve many of the trivial many. The focus would now be on the vital few. Any energies directed toward other problems were wasteful unless the committee substituted a new problem for one of the vital few. Pat had hoped the steering committee would have focused more on learning defects, but she was pleased with the start. The principal of Quality Land Middle School had told her that it would take time for the steering committee to focus on customer problems instead of problems more associated with teacher concerns. She would have to continually remind the steering committee of their mission to improve student learning.

The steering committee developed a system identification table for each of the vital few problems. Each problem was stated in project statement form. Analyzing the system identification tables, the steering committee selected "Lack of Parent Involvement" as the first quality opportunity, although it received the third-most votes. The steering committee believed that making an impact in parental involvement would have the greatest benefit to the school. The project statement read: "Increase the number of parents volunteering and attending conferences and parent/teacher nights." The system identification table for this opportunity follows.

Project Statement	Authority for Final Decision	Process Owners	Process	Customers	Suppliers	Value to Customer	Timing for Solution	Trend
Increase the number of parents volunteering, attending conferences and parent nights.	Steering committee	Teachers Students	Involving parents	Parents Staff	Prinicipal Consultants	High	This school year	Stable

The steering committee chartered a customer/supplier team. The charter read as shown on page 100.

The customer/supplier team met one hour each week for a semester. The team's use of the QPC tools will be addressed in the next chapter.

PAT TRIES REALITY THERAPY

A new way of looking at data unfolded for Pat as she began keeping control charts on several processes—student absences, teacher absences, and student learning defects (as evidenced by the number of D's and F's per teacher). While examining the data on teacher absences, she discovered a special cause: James Goodwin, whose absences were out of control. Pat scheduled a conference with James in which she planned to examine the data and determine reasons for absences. Pat

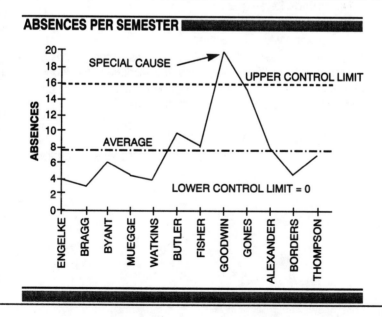

ABSENCES PER SEMESTER

CHARTER FOR QUALITY BREAKTHROUGH TEAM
TYPE: Customer/Supplier Team
CHARTERED BY: Trail's End CIM Steering Committee

I. STATEMENT OF PURPOSE AND RATIONALE FOR CHARTER: *(Why was this problem selected?)*

There is a need to increase parent involvement in the school. The data show that less than 20 parents volunteered last year. Parent conferences have been discontinued for lack of interest. Parent visitation night attracts fewer than 10 percent of the parents.

II. SCOPE OF TEAM: *(Cost and personnel restrictions)*

The team should not consider additional personnel. All other requests will be considered.

III. PROJECT STATEMENT AND EXPECTED RESULTS:

Increase the number of parent volunteers, parent conferences, and parents attending parent night in involving parents in the school.

(Does the charter give appropriate guidance to the team?)

IV. TEAM COMPOSITION (5–8 members):

TEAM SPONSOR—Don Owens

TEAM CHAIRPERSON—To be selected

TEAM FACILITATOR—Will Survive

TEAM MEMBERS:

1. Margaret Daugherty—parent
2. Margaret Salinas—parent
3. Belinda Pruneda—parent
4. Brenda Lera—parent
5. Kat Baldwin—teacher
6. Susan Wilcox—teacher

(Are there representatives from all groups in the process? Did the team get input from managers and workers in the process?)

Attach flow charts, control charts, Pareto Diagrams, cause–effect diagrams, etc., used in planning the charter.

RECOMMENDED PLAN FOR ACTION

STRATEGY	EXPECTED OUTCOME	RESPONSIBLE PERSON(S)
1.		
2.		
3.		
4.		
5.		

preplanned how she would give James constructive feedback and avoid criticism. If the absences were explainable, then the conference would be brief. If a problem was found, Pat would use what she knew of reality therapy counseling to develop a plan for improvement.

The conference was held the next day, during James' conference period. The data showed that James was absent every Friday. When Pat asked him to explain the data, James' response was that he often felt overwhelmed by his disruptive students, so he called in sick on Fridays. Pat asked him if being absent on Fridays was solving the larger problem of disruptive students. James agreed it did not solve anything, but it helped him cope. Pat asked James if he wanted to try to solve the problem. He did, but was afraid to try. After discussing James' classroom management style and recalling her walk-through inspections of the class, it became apparent that James could use help in organizing more efficiently. Pat asked James if he would attend a district cooperative learning training session. He agreed to do this. Pat told him that she would help him plan a week's unit built around a cooperative learning unit. They agreed to try it for one week, and then get together to assess the unit. Pat asked James to record each day on a check sheet the number of student misbehaviors. The conference ended positively, with James expressing hope for the first time in years.

TEACHER WILL E. SURVIVE

Will was happy to be asked to serve on the customer/supplier team organized to study parent involvement on campus. He felt this experience would help him to both use the QPC tools and transfer their use to his classroom. He was already using cause–effect diagrams with the students to brainstorm causes for lack of quality learning. The class used the Ten–Four Consensus Voting and Pareto Diagram to determine the vital problems to solve. These were: (1) Instruction/knowledge is not relevant; (2) Grades do not indicate mastery; and (3) Need for more explanation. Will chartered a team of students to take each vital cause and come back with recommendations. He agreed to facilitate the team.

Will began keeping charts on the number of students needing tutoring each week. This would indicate how many students did not understand the content after initial instruction. Before each unit of study, Will conducted a quality circle on the usefulness of the subject matter. This helped him plan concepts that students saw as useful. He used the Six Hats to examine issues in the unit.

Classroom behaviors had improved in Will's class since students had become more involved in the learning. Students also were doing homework at night to improve their understanding. Will would accept only competent or quality work, with quality defined as one step above competent. More students were striving for quality work than ever before. But then there was Rodney, Will's special cause. He did not need to chart the misbehaviors: Rodney was out of control every day. Will decided to have a conference with Rodney.

Will's plan was to use reality therapy. He started the conference by asking if Rodney was having any problems. Rodney refused to talk. Will realized that he and Rodney had established very little trust, so he decided to drop the focus on problems and have a conversation about Rodney's likes and dislikes. The conversation lasted several minutes—long enough for Rodney to reveal that his parents were getting divorced. Will also discovered that Rodney liked skate boarding. He ended the conference by asking Rodney to bring his skate board to school, to show him how he did it.

Will scheduled a second conference with Rodney. He was convinced that Rodney was controlling for belonging and love. He knew he could not substitute for Rodney's parents, but he could be a friend. Will called Rodney's parents to ask for their help. He did not mention Rodney's misbehavior, saying only that their son needed more attention at home. During the actual conference, Will continued to build trust. He asked Rodney's advice on class problems, and Rodney responded with several good ideas. (After all, Will thought, everyone likes to be asked for advice.)

In the third conference, Will felt it was time to talk about Rodney's class problems. The conference went as follows.

Step 1: Evaluate/Focus

Will: *What were you doing in class today?*

Rodney: *Nothing!*

Will: *I am asking about the problem with Jim.*

Rodney: *I wasn't doing anything. Jim called me a name.*

Will: *What did you do?*

Rodney: *I hit him with my pencil. He deserved it.*

Will: *And that is when I requested you to move to the cooling-off area, right?*

Rodney:	*Yes. Why didn't you get on Jim? He started it!*
Will:	*Let's solve your problems first. How many squabbles have you been in with classmates in the last two weeks? Three or four, correct?*
Rodney:	*Yeah, I guess that's right. But the others pick on me.*
Will:	*What do you do to cause them to pick on you?*
Rodney:	*Nothing. Well I guess I don't like to be teased. They call me names like "pig head."*
Will:	*When you fight back does that solve the problem?*
Rodney:	*Yes, at least for that day.*
Will:	*Would you like to figure out how to keep them from calling you names for more than one day?*
Rodney:	*That would be good. But there's nothing I can do. They don't like me.*
Will:	*What could you do different the next time one calls you a name?*
Rodney:	*I guess I could ignore him.*
Will:	*That would be different, but would it work?*
Rodney:	*No, they would probably think I was a sissy.*
Will:	*Could you do something in class so they wouldn't think of you as a pig head? What is a pig head, anyway?*
Rodney:	*They think I'm stupid.*
Will:	*What do you do in class that makes them think you are stupid?*
Rodney:	*Well, I'm not stupid. I haven't done my work in your class because I think it's stupid.*
Will:	*Are you calling my class a pig head? Just joking. You are pretty smart. What would it take for you to show how smart you are in class?*
Rodney:	*I could do the work, but I haven't felt like it lately.*
Will:	*Are you talking about your mother and father?*
Rodney:	*Yes—you know they're getting a divorce.*
Will:	*Yes. How will not doing work in class help what is happening at home?*
Rodney:	*When I'm angry I can't concentrate on my work.*
Will:	*Is getting angry helping you solve your problems?*
Rodney:	*No, but what else can I do?*
Will:	*Would you agree that when you choose anger it ends up with you in trouble for squabbling or not doing your work?*

Rodney:	I guess so. But, I don't choose anger, it just comes over me when I think about my parents.

Step 2: Plan/Commitment

Will:	The first time you found out about your parents, you experienced a pure feeling of anger. But it lasted only a short time. Since then you have chosen anger to deal with your problems. What could you choose instead of anger?
Rodney:	I could joke with the other students. I guess I could even laugh about the name calling.
Will:	If I called you a pig head now, how would you laugh it off?
Rodney:	I would say I guess I am sometimes but so is everyone. Then I'd laugh.
Will:	Could you do that tomorrow in class?
Rodney:	Yeah!
Will:	Will you do that in class tomorrow?
Rodney:	I'll try.
Will:	No, I am not asking whether you will try. I am asking if you will choose joking or laughter instead of anger. This means a lot to me.
Rodney:	OK. I'll do it from now on, when they tease me.
Will:	I am just asking for tomorrow or the next time someone teases you.
Rodney:	I can do anything once. I'll do it.

Step 3: Practice/Recycle

Will:	That's great. I want to talk with you on Friday to see how it went. We'll make plans for the rest of the six weeks. I want us to discuss ways you can stop angering and do work in class.
Rodney:	I'll see you at lunch on Friday.

Rodney had been acting out for some time, so Will did not expect him to change overnight. That is why Will focused on changing Rodney's behavior with the other students first; Rodney quickly needed to experience a small success. If the plan worked, then Will could begin concentrating on helping Rodney change angering as a chosen behavior, to working in class. He would pick an assignment in which Rodney would probably be successful. If Will recognized this success with

Rodney's peers, the name-calling would probably stop. Will could then plan with Rodney how the young man could deal with his troubled home life. "People do not fail, only plans fail." If there were to be setbacks, it was important that Rodney experience the consequences. However, Rodney must know that Will was not going to give up on him. A better plan was needed.

Will built trust between himself and Rodney first. If trust is present, the situation usually will improve even if the teacher does not do a good job with the use of reality therapy. However, with practice, teachers and counselors can learn to focus on the behavior and wants of the problematical student. Then, it is only natural to ask the student to evaluate where his or her chosen behavior is leading. It is important that students see that all of their behaviors are chosen. Many students blame other students, or teachers or parents, for their own behavior. Once the student recognizes that his or her behavior is only causing the problem to get worse, then it is time to plan. But the plan must be the student's, not the counselor's.

Will asked Rodney if he could try out their agreed-on behavior on the next class day. It is important to practice the newly chosen behavior as soon as possible. A commitment to "do it tomorrow" will be more acceptable, and have the greater chance of success, than a commitment for the rest of the month, or six weeks. Will was not about to accept a maybe when he asked "Will you do it?" And he never asked Rodney why his pupil chose anger. That would only teach Rodney to make excuses for his behavior. When Rodney had offered excuses for his behavior, Will politely but firmly refused them. And he asked for a *plan*. Students must learn to not make excuses, but rather better plans for their lives that will eliminate the *need* for excuses. Will guarded against making value judgements *for* Rodney, knowing that Rodney needed to discover what his anger was causing.

Will would not have had the time to work with this Rodney if there had been other Rodneys in class. Conferencing using reality therapy counseling should be used with the student experiencing the *most* difficulty in class. *All* teachers have time to work to build trust with at least one student in each class. Will's implementation of the quality approach in his class should eliminate most of the other nonproductive behavior.

SYSTEM FEEDBACK

Supplier	→	Input	→	Process	→	Output Product/ Service	→	Customers
Data collectors		Control charts Histograms Customer surveys Performance Goals Indexes Organizational health data		Identifying quality opportunities		Problem system identification Project state- ment Team charter type and charter		Chartered team

In a quality school or school district, administrators are lead managers. This management style implies that evaluations, rankings, averaging, and other management-by-results activities are eliminated. The fear that these activities introduce into the system is self-defeating, producing win–lose situations. Allowing those closest to the processes to assess their own quality and improve it is the quality way. However, administrators must exercise some control over these processes—otherwise, they would never know that special causes exist and need to be explained. Control means keeping data on the important processes in the system, which is why administrators should keep control charts, performance goal indexes, organizational health data, and other data. The role of administrators is to focus the steering committee or management team on defects, waste, and common causes in the system. No longer does management solve the problems; focusing the process owners on the problem is the more appropriate and productive role. Management then gives them the information, resources, and authority to solve the problem. Management should train the steering committee or management team to collect data and study the data for quality opportunities. At this stage, management should step in only when the customer is ignored. It is common for teams in the early stages of empowerment to focus more on the welfare of team members than on the customer. Management must remind the team of their mission, and focus on satisfying the needs of the customer.

Mass inspection at the end of the line is costly and does not produce quality. However, some inspection should occur at the output stage. Inspecting a representative sample of the output will provide sufficient feedback for checking quality. Mass inspection should not be removed until process owners are using the QPC tools to improve the quality of their process. When the mass inspection begins to show that the system is producing quality outputs, then mass inspection can be eliminated. For example, testing all the students at the end of the year with a criterion test may be necessary until students begin scoring in the quality range. As quality concepts are implemented, however, testing a sample of students at the end of the year may suffice. At some point, management may see no need for any end-of-the-line testing. This decision should occur after several years of improving processes to the point where quality is a given. Everyone will know when that day has come. Then there will be no need for rework rooms or recycling of students. The cost of inspection can be applied to a lower pupil–teacher ratio, higher salaries, or better benefits. It is important for process owners to see cost-saving due to quality returned to the workers.

THE DICKINSON EXPERIENCE

Each spring in the Dickinson Independent School District, the administrative team identifies the quality opportunities on which to focus energies for the next school year. The team examines the data collected during the year, then uses the QPC tools to isolate the vital few problems to study. Teams are then chartered to solve the problems over the course of the school year. This system differs radically from the "old" way of solving problems, which was in effect to not solve any problems at all. Instead, administrators attempted to focus their individual efforts on the gamut of dilemmas facing the system each year, collaborating only when a problem reared its head and could no longer be ignored. The result was that no problems got solved, but a lot of flames got snuffed out temporarily. Using CIM, management must resist the temptation to get back into the firefighting business. The team must stay focused on the vital few problems. Only when the management team agrees by consensus should a "new" one be added to the vital few agenda.

In Dickinson, each campus and support department's management team begins the year with the vital few problems for the campus or department already identified. Using the tools, every team in the system is focused on those that will make the most impact on improving quality. This is not to say that the trivial many are not addressed. Chapter 10 shows how the trivial many are solved.

MANAGEMENT PRINCIPLES USED

ORGANIZING

Creating breakthrough teams for problem-solving.

PLANNING

Identify quality opportunities:

1. Analyze data on defects, waste, and customer satisfaction.

2. Brainstorm quality opportunities, using a cause–effect diagram.

3. Group similar opportunities and list them.

4. Use consensus-gathering tools.

5. Use the Pareto principle to select the vital few problems to study.

6. Use Six Hats to identify components of the vital few problems.

7. Complete a system identification table on each problem.

8. Decide on a type of team needed to solve the vital few problems.

CONTROLLING

1. Check the Pareto diagram for consensus.

2. Check system identification for the importance of the problem.

LEADING

1. Delegate authority to chartered teams.

2. Identify, explain, and correct special causes.

3. Use constructive feedback and reality therapy conferencing with special-cause personnel problems.

Continuous Improvement of Quality

The distinctive mark of a CIM organization is teamwork. Where once a lone manager held sway, firing off decisions at the rate of a .45 automatic, there exist teams whose members collect data, analyze information, brainstorm solutions, and reach consensus. As in the example of Trail's End Middle School in Chapter 6, teams are typically chartered, or authorized, by a higher-level team to take charge of a particular problem or to improve a process. Chartered teams are short-lived work units designed to obtain a breakthrough and then to disband. In a fully functioning CIM organization, any group of process owners (customers and suppliers to the process) can request a team charter to solve a problem they have identified. The only prerequisites are that the team has investigated the process using the proper tools, and has determined that there are defects that can be eliminated. Cost parameters are typically the major limiting factor to the scope of teams in organizations that have truly moved decision-making to the level closest to the process.

One problem-solving structure used by process improvement teams is called the Team Approach to Problem Solving (TAPS). TAPS is designed using the QPC tools and an improvement outline based on the Shewhart Cycle of plan-do-check/study-act. Process improvement teams and customer/supplier teams alike focus on improving a process; the difference in the teams is their composition. Process owners constitute most, if not all, of the members of process improvement teams. They obtain feedback from the customers and suppliers of the process, but the problem is left to the process owners to solve. Customer/supplier teams are composed of customers and suppliers of a process that is producing a defect or waste which is causing problems for both parties. For example, transporting students is a process owned by transportation department workers. A defect of the process is bus misbehavior by students. This defect impacts both the campus and the bus drivers. It cannot be solved without problem-solving teamwork by the customer (school administration) and the supplier (bus drivers). Examples of other common customer/supplier problems that occur in schools are yard maintenance, which often causes safety and noise problems for teachers and students; defects in student curriculum occurring in a previous grade and not corrected in the grade thereafter; and communication gaps or misunderstandings between administration and employees.

The TAPS model used by process improvement teams and customer/supplier teams is a seven-step process:

Step 1: Collect System Data

1. Collect system data on the product/service of the process to be studied:
   a. Control charts
   b. Histograms
   c. Check Sheets
   d. Performance goal indices
   e. Graphs
2. Survey the customer's and supplier's expectations and requirements:
   a. Face-to-face discussions
   b. Telephone interviews
   c. Observations
   d. Surveys
3. Brainstorm using the Six Hats tool.

Step 2: Analyze the Process

1. Develop a process flow diagram.
2. Analyze and make structural and procedural changes.

Step 3: Identify Vital Causes

1. Develop a cause-and-effect diagram.
2. Clarify and categorize causes.
3. Use Ten–Four voting or the Delphi Technique to reach consensus.
4. Develop a Pareto diagram for showing consensus of the vital few causes.

Step 4: Collect Data on The Vital Few Causes

1. Check the process flow diagram to determine where measurements should take place for the cause selected.
2. Determine the measurement system:
   a. Control charts
   b. Histograms
   c. Check sheets
   d. Other
3. Collect data.

Step 5: Analyze Data and Determine Improvement Strategies

1. Study data and develop fact statements.
2. Use Six Hats to arrive at a solution.
3. Try it on a limited scale—pilot or field study.

Step 6: Monitor and Assess

1. Determine a measurement system for pilot or field study:
   a. Control charts
   b. Histograms
   c. Check sheets
   d. Regression graphs
2. Monitor data.
3. Assess for results.

Step 7: Decide and Act

Decision-making:

1. If data are inconclusive, then select the next vital cause, or revise the plan for the vital cause and repeat the cycle.

2. If a pilot or field study is successful, then present recommendations to the parent committee. Include the following in the presentation:

   a. Project statement

   b. Process flow diagram

   c. Cause-and-effect diagram

   d. Pareto diagram

   e. Data

      (1) Control charts

      (2) Histograms

      (3) Check sheets

      (4) Other data formats

   f. Action Plan

      (1) Objectives

      (2) Strategies

      (3) What, who, when, where, and how?

   g. Recommendation

USING THE 7-STEP CYCLE AND PLAN-DO-CHECK-ACT

A chartered team should begin by analyzing the project statement and charter to specifically determine the task and limits. The facilitator should lead the team in selecting a chairperson for developing the agenda and for setting the date, time, and place of every meeting. The team also should select a recorder for keeping team minutes and summarizing at the end of the meetings. Other roles can be selected at the option of the team. By collecting data outside of meeting time and by limiting meeting conversation to the topic, teams can meet their objectives even if they meet only once a week. The hour should be spent using the tools. This is not a typical committee meeting, but rather a team meeting designed to solve a problem.

The first step is collecting system data. At the first meeting, assignments should be made by the chairperson for the collection of input, output, process, and customer data on the problem

CONTINUOUS IMPROVEMENT CYCLE

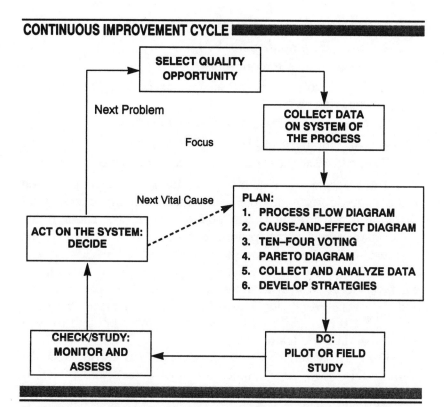

to be solved. The second meeting should be devoted to using the Six Hats to get a clearer understanding of the problem. (The Six Hats are explained in Chapter 6.)

The next step for the team is to develop a process-flow diagram of the process as it currently functions. It is important that the process-flow diagram reflect the actual process rather than the ideal. When teams develop a process-flow diagram that reflects the ideal, they are in effect proposing solutions before analyzing problems. If the team is in doubt as to parts of the process it should ask the workers who own the process. If the team finds it difficult to diagram the process it may indicate an unnecessarily complex or inefficient process structure. Unfortunately, many school processes are ill-defined and variable; the process operates differently depending on circumstances. This indicates a need to develop a more defined process. To refine or improve the process the team should examine the process-flow diagram for the following characteristics.

Here is a checklist for analyzing the process:

1. Are there too many steps?
2. Can it be simplified?
3. Are there any rework loops?
4. Are there any mass inspections or end-of-the-line checking steps?
5. Are there too many decision-making steps?
6. Can time be saved by paralleling steps?
7. Are there activities that do not add value to the customer?

The diagram and resultant procedures should be improved at the stage during which the team discovers inefficiencies. After changing procedures, it is advisable to collect data to determine if the change has in fact produced a better product. If not, the problem-solving process should continue, using the TAPS model. For example, a team investigating ways to improve data-reporting procedures in a district may create a process flow diagram and discover several duplications of effort. Once the loops are eliminated, the system's efficiency may improve enough to warrant disbanding the team.

Once an accurate process flow diagram is constructed, the team should begin to examine causes of defects and waste by using a fishbone or cause-and-effect diagram. The process flow diagram will give the team clues as to where causes may exist in the process. The team should discuss each cause generated, or use the Six Hats tool. Any of the consensus-gathering tools may be used for consensus. The Ten–Four Voting tool is useful if the team has time during a meeting to go through the procedure. When meeting time is scarce, use the Delphi Technique to prioritize. (The Delphi can even be done through interoffice mail.) After the results are tabulated, a Pareto diagram should be constructed, in order to determine the vital few causes to study. The team should decide whether to study either one cause, or all of them together.

In the data-collecting step, the team should examine the process flow diagram for parts of the process related to the vital few causes. The team should determine how to collect data at the various points in the process. Collecting data on the causes is important because it will give the team a benchmark to examine when the corrections are applied. It will also give an indication of the degree to which the cause is affecting the process. Cause data are collected from parts of the process that may be causing the problem. Control charts, check sheets, and surveys are some of the measurement tools that can be used. The team needs to determine who will collect the data, as well as where, when, and what will be collected. The team should keep the monitoring process as simple as possible, keeping in mind that some causes may be quite difficult to measure. Observation by the team members or a process owner may provide written anecdotal data that can be used.

Once enough data are collected, it is time for the team to develop consensus on a strategy for improvement. The strategy often becomes obvious to the team when the data point in a particular direction. If that doesn't happen, the team should use the Six Hats tool to clarify the meaning of the data, and brainstorm corrective alternatives. After Six Hats, the team should reach consensus through voting, and then develop a Pareto diagram to view the major causes. The team should develop an action plan by listing the strategies, the person responsible for each strategy, when it will be implemented, and where it will be applied. This completes the *planning* stage of the TAPS method.

Now the team needs to *do* it. The team should implement the strategies on a trial basis, or in a pilot process, for a specified length of time. This gives the team a chance to study or check the results and make corrections. The team should determine how it will measure the success or failure of the pilot. Once the pilot is completed, the data are analyzed to determine the next action. The data will determine one of the following actions:

1. The pilot is an improvement over the existing process, so the team should act on the system to change it. Develop the recommendations to present to the parent committee.

2. Data are inconclusive, so the team must make a decision as to whether to continue the pilot/trial or study another cause.

3. Data indicate that the pilot does not improve the process. Move to the next vital cause.

The presentation to the parent committee should include all charts and diagrams, an action plan, and a recommendation. Because the team recommendation comes from those representing the process, the parent committee should approve the recommendation if the tools have been used properly and the data appear solid. The parent committee should never change the recommendation, although they may send it back to the breakthrough team for restudy if specific, legitimate concerns are raised.

PITFALLS

Numerous pitfalls line the paths that teams follow in using the TAPS method. Teams should therefore guard against starting with solutions, as it is tempting to throw them at any unexpected problem. The team must start with causes, rather than solutions. To do otherwise, even when a solution seems obvious, is to put the cart before the horse. Sometimes the horse will be able to push rather than pull the cart, but when that happens it is always an exception. (So is quality decision-making a rarity when a team begins with solutions.)

Another pitfall occurs when teams fail to get consensus; all decisions must be by consensus. The team must agree on how to achieve consensus, and then use the tools to act on it. Consensus is not total agreement of each member concerning a decision, but rather team agreement to support the decision. The distinction is crucial! Team members must arrive at a decision to support the direction of the team, even though it may signify personal compromise. But if all team members are involved in the use of the tools, achieving consensus rarely is difficult.

When using a cause-and-effect diagram, it is important to make sure the effect is related to the project statement. When the project statement and effect do not match, the team may be seeking causes that have little or no relation to the problem. Not grouping like causes on a fishbone will create a splitting of consensus votes or rankings. This will create a situation similar to one in which two candidates, both with identical platforms, run against each other and a third candidate who holds differing views. Voters may split their preference between the lookalikes, allowing the third candidate to win. The team should avoid confusion in the Ten–Four Voting by taking the time to clarify any of the brainstormed ideas. The Six Hats works well for this. The team members must take time to study all of the possible causes, since to do otherwise creates the pitfall of a no-consensus Pareto in which the members vote for their ideas only.

Foundational to good team decision-making are reliable, accurate, and timely measurement tools. Faulty data-gathering techniques can create false solutions. The measurement tools should be simple, economical, and practical: Collecting the data should not require excessive time. The team needs to make the following decisions when collecting data:

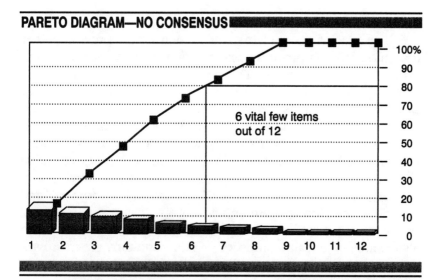

PARETO DIAGRAM—NO CONSENSUS

6 vital few items
out of 12

100%
90
80
70
60
50
40
30
20
10
0

1 2 3 4 5 6 7 8 9 10 11 12

1. **Why:** Will correcting the selected cause fulfill the project statement?
2. **What:** Errors, defects, failures, etc.
3. **Where:** In the process and at the end of the process
4. **When:** As it happens or after it happens
5. **How much:** 100 percent or sample size
6. **How to assemble:** Develop a format

Another data-collection pitfall to avoid is measuring the cause in the wrong location. Using the process flow diagram should prevent this from happening.

Finally, the team must avoid piloting the change on too large a scale. The team can easily lose control of a large project. If the wrong cause was selected, it will be difficult to shut off a large-scale project.

The work is not accomplished once the parent committee approves the corrective strategies; two major tasks await. First, the parent committee must insure that the recommendations are implemented on the system. This can be done by chartering an implementation team to get the plan into action across the organization. Second, the parent committee must establish a monitoring system for the new process, to determine if the strategies are working to improve the process and will continue to do so. Control charts are effective monitoring methods because problems can be noted while the process is in action.

DESIGN TEAMS

The task of many teams is to design a new process, rather than modify or improve an existing one. In that case, a design team should be chartered. This team will deviate from the TAPS model outlined above because there is no process to analyze for causes; the team must create a new process. Two major questions must be addressed: "What will the product or service be?" and "How will the product or service be delivered?" A separate team might be needed for each, with different types of members. The team chartered to design the product or service may be composed of top decision-makers, internal customers, and suppliers. The "how" team should consist of those who would be the new process owners. However, it may be productive to also charter one team composed of administrators, process owners, and internal customers and suppliers. The eight-step design model is as follows.

Product/Service Design

1. Collect internal and external customer needs and requirements.
2. Develop criteria for the design.
3. Decide on a format and develop product or service features.
4. Develop a performance goal index.

Process Design

5. Develop process features.
6. Pilot the new process.
7. Collect data and analyze.
8. Act on the system by implementing the new process throughout operations.

The design team organizes in the same manner as a chartered breakthrough team. Once roles are determined, the team needs to begin collecting data from customers. The system-identification data will help determine who the customers are. Internal and external customer input is vital to developing the new product or service features. Questions that should be asked of the customer include:

1. Why is a new product or service needed?
2. What are your expectations of the new product or service?
3. What would be your standard of quality for the product or service?
4. What would cause you to brag about the product or service?

Data gathered from the customer surveys and interviews will provide bits and pieces of information that must be translated into statements of criteria for the design. Criteria statements are requirements of the customer as stated by the design team. Examples in education include "The curriculum should be competency-based," "The program requires safety training," and "The discipline system provides counseling for students to help them choose more appropriate behaviors." The next task for the team is to select a format for the features. The facilitator should ask team members what would best describe, in process owners' language, the finished product or service. The formats might be policy statements, procedures, a process flow diagram, a drawing, or a model. Once the format is selected, the team should brainstorm the features of the product by using the criteria. If the format is a set of procedures, then a team should develop the sequential directions accompanying the procedures. By this stage, the team has finished the "what" of the design and is ready to produce the finished product or service. Before moving to this task, the team needs to develop indicators that will measure the quality of the product or service as it is used or delivered. The indicators can be presented in a performance goal index. At least one index should reflect customer satisfaction.

The process for delivering the product or service begins with brainstorming the activities and decisions involved therein. The procedures can be written on sticky notes, for ease in placing and replacing in the development of a process flow diagram. Each procedure should be tested for customer value added. The procedure should add value to the design of the product or service, as measured by the customer's needs. The final PFD should be analyzed, using the criteria explained in the description of process flow diagraming. The team should translate the final PFD procedures into policies, directives, blueprints, and/or directions for operations. The design procedures should be tried out in a pilot or field test. The team should decide on the measurement criteria, and methods of collecting the data, for the pilot or field test. The measurement criteria should reflect customer needs. The data should be analyzed, and a decision made to either act on the system or redesign the procedures to eliminate causes of defects, waste, or procedures that do not add value. The TAPS model can be used to improve the process of increasing customer satisfaction. When the design procedures are ready, either an implementation team can be chartered or the procedures can be transferred to operations. The customers should be involved in examining the final products or services.

PRINCIPAL PAT ANN HOLD

Pat was excited about the prospect of facilitating a breakthrough team on management of student behavior. She knew that all eyes would be on her as she started the school down the road of team-based decision-making. This was an excellent opportunity to demonstrate that systematic problem-solving is worth the time and effort, she thought. The team was composed of teachers, the assistant principal, and a handful of students. They all arrived at the following project statement: "To decrease the number of students sent to the office for the second time for irresponsible student actions." The team used the Six Hats to brainstorm the issue and decide on the data it would need to collect in order to understand the problem. They selected the following data to gather:

1. Control chart of number of students sent to the office per teacher, per week, and for the second time
2. Survey of teacher and student perceptions of school discipline
3. Available research on school discipline trends
4. Number of suspensions during the year

Pat facilitated the team in constructing a process flow diagram of the actual current process for managing student behavior.

By analyzing the diagram, the team discovered two problems: no consistency in classroom management practices, and no preventive measures. The team discussed ways to teach students responsibility, and how to structure a noncoercive discipline system. Pat led the team in constructing a cause-and-effect diagram. The causes were grouped together, and discussed using the Six Hats. The team reached a consensus on the following vital few

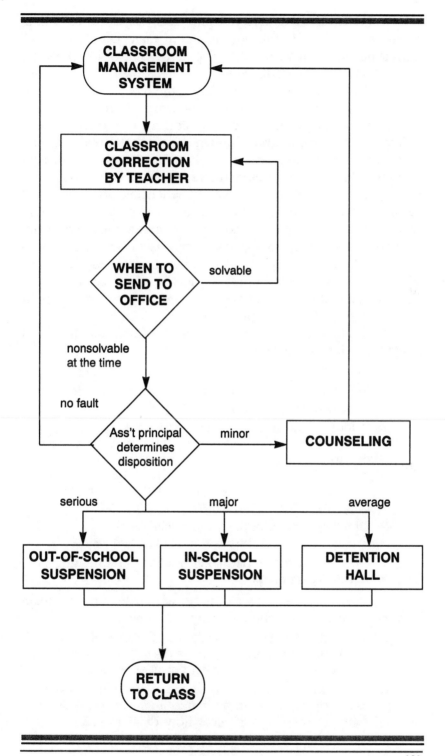

causes: (1) Home and personal problems; (2) Coercive school environment; and (3) Lack of classroom management training. Correcting these causes would solve 80 percent of the problem, according to the Pareto diagram.

Pat helped the team to brainstorm the type of data it would need to collect on the vital causes. The team referred to the flow diagram to determine where to collect the information. Collecting information about student home backgrounds would require personal interviews and discussions with the Student Assistance Program counselor. The result would be a profile portraying characteristics of a student experiencing home and personal problems. Measuring the degree of coercion in the system was another big challenge; coercion was something the team members agreed was so subtle at times as to be almost unnoticeable. The team finally decided to use a perception survey of students who had been referred to the office for discipline problems. Finally, the teachers were surveyed to determine their level of classroom management training.

A month later, the team met to analyze the data. It arrived at the following conclusions:

1. Two out of five students were from single parent homes.
2. About 25 percent of the students were experiencing serious home problems.
3. Students who had been referred to the office for discipline matters did not believe there was an alternative to the punishment they received for their offenses. The committee believed that this was the reason for the high rate of second and third visits to the office by the same students.
4. Only ten percent of the teachers had taken a classroom management workshop within the last five years.
5. Only five teachers had taken multicultural training or sensitivity training.

After discussion, brainstorming, and research, the team arrived at consensus on the following recommendations:

1. A parent training course would be offered to all parents, but made mandatory for parents of students involved in more than one minor or major behavior problem.
2. The school would create a new discipline system based on reality therapy counseling. The procedures were outlined in a process flow diagram created by

the team. The new discipline system developed by the team contained the following ten steps.

Preventive Measures

1. Develop student ownership in the school:
   a. All teachers should involve students in developing both standards and a mission statement for each class.
   b. All students must know the school rules and their responsibilities to operate within the rules.
   c. All students and teachers must learn lead management, control theory, and reality therapy principles.
2. Teachers should conduct a quality circle meeting at least once every two weeks.
3. The school should become a friendly and noncoercive place for students:
   a. Everyone should be courteous.
   b. Students with problems will be assigned a mentor advocate.
   c. Teachers should attempt to satisfy student needs for fun, recognition, belonging, and choices.

Classroom Correction

4. Teachers are encouraged to use their own ingenuity to stop misconduct:
   a. Do what usually works—but if it does not work, stop doing it.
   b. Build trust with negative class leaders.
   c. Use reality therapy counseling.
   d. Start fresh each day with all students.
5. Initiate a conference with the most irresponsible student in the class who is causing problems:
   a. Use reality therapy to focus on present behavior and the student's need.
   b. Evaluate present behavior.
   c. Develop a plan.
   d. Get student commitment to follow the plan on a trial basis.

e. Schedule a practice period and follow-up conference to assess results.

f. Satisfy student's need. Example: give a class "bully" who is striving for power a classroom role that satisfies this need.

6. Use a Quiet Area for those showing continued misbehavior:

a. Do not accept excuses.

b. Do not set time limits.

c. Give students a choice to stay in the Quiet Area or to initiate a conference with the teacher.

d. Conduct a conference, using reality therapy principles.

(1) Hold a conference during last five minutes of class.

(2) Issue a conference pass that other teachers will honor.

e. Call parents if student is sent to Quiet Area a second time.

f. Use Quiet Area at least three times before moving to Step 7.

Office Correction

7. Send the student to the office if classroom mediation is not working and irresponsible conduct is depriving others (including the teacher) of their needs:

a. Be noncoercive and develop trust.

b. Conference with the student to build a plan to eliminate past excuses and causes.

c. Assign consequences, giving the student choices.

d. Recycle to Step 6, show the plan developed in Step 7b to the teacher and work the problem out in the Quiet Area.

e. Call the parents for a conference.

8. Assign the student to the counseling center for an indefinite time:

a. A counseling-center aide will help the student to develop a better plan.

b. The student must complete assignments.

c. The student schedules a conference with the teacher when ready.

d. If the conference is successful, then recycle to Step 4.

e. If the conference is not successful, call the parents and request a meeting with them.

f. Use the counseling center at least three times before Step 9.

9. Assign a Tolerance Day if any student continues to not work:

a. Never give up on students.

b. Hold a reentry conference in the counseling center in order to develop a plan for appropriate behavior.

c. Recycle to Step 8.

d. Have parent come with student for conference. Include parent in conference with student to develop a better plan that eliminates past failures.

e. Use Tolerance Day at least three times before moving to Step 10.

10. Seek outside expertise only as a last resort:

a. Conduct a meeting of teachers and counselors, to determine causes.

b. Determine a solution, including special programs, modifications, and/or other remedies.

c. Recycle to Step 8 and review with the student the new plan developed by the committee.

3. The school should develop a training program to introduce teachers to the new system. The training should cover successful classroom management practices, reality therapy counseling, Quality Circles, and trust-building skills. Conduct a workshop in multicultural sensitivity.

4. The school should offer group counseling to students experiencing home and personal problems. The groups should address the problems determined in the data collection.

An action plan was developed for each recommendation. The team also developed trial tests for each recommendation, and a plan for data collection.

After the pilot period, the team analyzed the data and decided whether to continue the trial tests with revisions, or to implement the plan across-the-board. The team also devised a system for monitoring the programs after implementation. Armed with charts and graphs to illustrate their data-collection results, the team presented the recommendations to the steering committee for approval. The steering committee approved all recommendations, giving the breakthrough team a great sense of accomplishment. Pat treated the team to dinner, to celebrate their success.

Recommendation	Trial system	Data to be collected	Where	When	Who	How
1. A parent training course	Select a group of parents to take course and evaluate it	Parent assessment	In the course	At the end	Instructor	Questionnaire
2. Noncoercive discipline system	Introduce in five phases with one grade level	1. Teacher perceptions	Classroom	At the end	Principal	Survey
		2. Student Perceptions	Grade level	At the end	Teachers	Survey
		3. Number of referrals	Office	Each week	Ass't principal	Control chart
		4. Second-time referrals	Office	At the end	Ass't principal	Check sheet
3. Develop training program	Offer to volunteer group of teachers	Assessment of training	In class	At the end	Instructor	Evaluation
4. Group counseling	Offer to one group of students	Student perceptions of group	In group	At the end	Group leader	Evaluation

TEACHER WILL E. SURVIVE

Will had been selected to facilitate the team chartered to study the problem of lack of parental involvement. The project statement read: "To increase the number of parent volunteers, parent conferences, and parents attending parent night in order to have greater involvement in school." Since there was no established process for parental involvement at Trail's End, Will knew he had a design problem on his hands. Or a design "quality opportunity," that is!

The chairperson began by assigning roles so that the team had a recorder, a timekeeper/task master, a data organizer, and a provider of such physical needs as snacks and refreshments. Will assigned to the members the task of collecting data from the customers, who in this case were the parents. A sampling of parents was asked what level of parental involvement they believed the school expected. The survey also asked parents what would be required to obtain greater parental involvement. The survey results were eye-opening, as parents indicated that the school lacked the inviting climate necessary for parental involvement. In particular, Hispanic parents felt ostracized from the school, commenting frequently on the lack of Spanish-language translators, and the frequent miscommunications that ensued. Will summarized the survey by stating that parents want to be involved, but must first feel welcome at and then must be able to participate in meaningful work.

Will facilitated a brainstorming session to develop criteria for performance goals with which to measure the success of the planned design. The general categories of criteria were:

1. Inviting and warm climate for parents
2. Effective communication with Hispanic parents
3. Meaningful involvement opportunities for parents

Using the criteria as effects, Will led the team in a cause-and-effect session to determine how to increase parent involvement. Consensus was reached by using the 5–3–1 rating system. Seventy-five percent agreement from the team members was to be considered consensus. The design pilot had the following features:

1. Greeter for visitors to campus
2. Badges for visitors
3. Survey of satisfaction to be given to parents after a visit
4. Assignment of a Hispanic aide to greet Hispanic parents
5. Development of a hot line manned by a Spanish-speaking aide, and an answering service in Spanish to answer questions for Spanish-speaking parents
6. Assignment of parents to classes in which to read, and listen to students read
7. Development of a lab in which to allow volunteers to work on reading difficulties with students. (Parents, community members, and business people would tutor students, under the direction of a teacher and an aide.)
8. Requirement that all teachers call their students' parents or guardians at least once each semester (A conference should be scheduled with any student making a grade of C or lower.)

The features were then translated into measurement criteria for a performance goal index. The performance criteria included the degree of parent satisfaction as measured by a parent survey; the number of parents visiting school per week; the number of Hispanic and other minority parents involved in school per week; a Spanish-language survey of Hispanic parents on school responsiveness; and the number of teachers using parents to help in the classroom. The criteria were then used to develop a performance goal index, which would indicate whether the team had been successful with their design.

The team also developed a written procedure or a process flow diagram for each service feature. For example, the procedures for the second recommendation were:

1. Develop a list of parent volunteers.
2. Make an ID badge for each person on list.
3. Make twenty extra badges for newcomers reading "Very Important Visitor".
4. Place badges at the front desk for visitors and volunteers.

The team developed a trial test for all recommendations, then analyzed the collected data on each test trial and made needed changes. They presented the procedures to the steering committee for approval, which was unanimous. Training sessions were held for those who would actually implement the procedures. Will agreed to monitor the performance goal index to assess the quality of the programs and new procedures. If problems occurred, he would inform the steering committee. Will was pleased (and relieved) that the intense teamwork had reached a fruitful conclusion. And the principal gave each team member a certificate of success, and a dinner for two at a local restaurant.

Flush with success from facilitating a design team, Will decided to introduce problem-solving to his classroom, on an upcoming unit on the Indian tribes of Texas. He would ditch the old method of lecture, followed by chapter-end questions that elicited murmuring responses from the students. Instead, Will developed a unit based on the TAPS model for problem-solving. First, he had to state a problem that would require students to research all the important data on Texas Indians, thus allowing students to understand important concepts.

PROBLEM-SOLVING UNIT

Problem: "How could the Indian policy pursued by the Texas and federal governments in the nineteenth century have been structured to preserve rather than disintegrate the Indian tribes as functioning units?"

Groups: Group students in fours. Allow students to appoint members for the roles of facilitator, taskmaster, recorder, and summarizer. The social skill to be monitored is cooperation.

1. **Identify the system:** Students will understand the system of Indian affairs policy-making used by the Texas and federal governments by identifying suppliers, input, process owners, output, and customers. Product would be a System Identification Table.

2. **Collect system data:** Students will conduct a Six Hats brainstorming session to arrive at sources and types of data to be collected by the team, so as to better understand the system and the problem. Encourage the team to put relevant data on charts and graphs.

3. **Survey the customers and suppliers:** The team could develop a survey for Indians living on a reservation in Texas, research the history of the tribes, and collect meaningful data. Suppliers would be the settlers and local government officials in nineteenth century Texas. (Such information is found in most school and public libraries in the state.)

4. **Analyze the process:** The team should develop a process flow diagram of the process for Indian policy development in the nineteenth century, using textbook information as base data.

5. **Identify vital causes:** Using their data and the flow diagram, the team should use a cause–effect diagram to brainstorm causes of the problem. The team should use Ten–Four consensus voting to arrive at agreement. A Pareto diagram should be constructed, to show the vital few causes and the degree of consensus.

6. **Collect data on the vital few causes:** Teams should check the process flow diagram to see where causes occur. Measurement criteria should be developed for determining the degree of cause. Criteria data should be collected by using the library and by interviewing local government officials on how to develop policy.

7. **Analyze data and determine improvement strategies:** The team should develop a fact statement related to the vital few causes. The team should use the Six Hats to arrive at possible solutions for the causes. The products should be a policy process and a statement that

would best solve the problem. The team should decide how the products would be tested on a trial basis.

8. **Monitor and assess:** The team should develop a quality assurance plan for monitoring the new policy and process. This would be an excellent place to introduce control charts to track such statistics as the number of policy violations per month, or Indian tribe population per month, as measures of stability.

9. **Act on the system:** The team must develop an action plan for implementing the new policy and policy process.

10. **Present the plan:** The team would need to present its plan to the class by using charts, graphs, and other data-viewing aids. All members must have a role in the presentation.

After the presentation, Will reflected on the changes that had occurred in his class. The problem-solving unit was a huge success, even though much of class time was devoted to teaching the tools. The students were noticeably more involved in the educational process as they worked on the team. It was as if for the first time a seemingly mundane issue, such as nineteenth century Indian policy, had become relevant in the 1990s. Most important to Will, the students were learning how to learn. They had been required to analyze processes, reach consensus, and present solutions—tasks that typically were not a part of classroom learning at Trail's End.

Will gained valuable feedback on the unit through a quality circle held a few days after the presentation. He confirmed that the students were strongly in favor of problem-solving units, and enjoyed cooperative efforts in general. For once, Will believed he had found a tool to make his subject interesting and relevant to students. As a result, he quickly began work on another problem-solving unit, appointing a team of four students to assist him in developing it. Eventually, Will began assigning two students per month to act as teacher assistants to develop visual aids, take care of clerical duties, and help develop tests.

In the following school year, Will formed a customer/supplier team organized to develop problem-solving units. Before each unit, he met with the entire class, to run through the design model showing how to develop what to teach, and how to deliver it to the students. Finally, Will and his students produced a problem-solving unit addressing a pressing campus problem, student vandalism. The students' recommendations were presented to the school management team, and accepted unanimously. Students voluntarily working together to solve school problems? Will pondered: A new day was at hand at Trail's End Middle School!

SYSTEM FEEDBACK

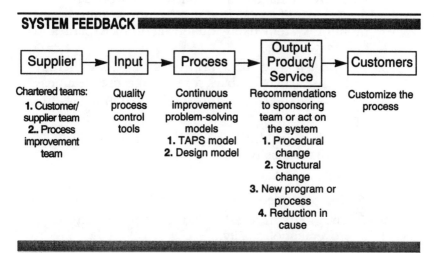

Supplier	Input	Process	Output Product/ Service	Customers
Chartered teams: **1.** Customer/ supplier team **2.** Process improvement team	Quality process control tools	Continuous improvement problem-solving models **1.** TAPS model **2.** Design model	Recommendations to sponsoring team or act on the system **1.** Procedural change **2.** Structural change **3.** New program or process **4.** Reduction in cause	Customize the process

THE DICKINSON EXPERIENCE

In the Dickinson ISD, most problems that merit attention are studied by first chartering a team. The success of the team is in the hands of the facilitator (no team should be allowed to function without a trained facilitator). Time should be allotted to the team for meetings. One hour a week is ample. The team should have a well-supplied meeting area, with easels and markers. An agenda should be sent to all members, along with the minutes of the last meeting, at least five days before the proposed meeting. At the end of the team meeting, someone should summarize the decisions made, and the assignments for the next meeting. An assessment of the meeting should take place either verbally or in written form. The sponsor assigned by the parent team or committee should report back the progress that the team is making. If there are problems, the sponsor should meet with the facilitator, to help solve them. Giving the team (say) $100 for supplies would be a good gesture that the parent team wants them to succeed. Sponsors should be prepared to cut red tape when necessary, in order to get needed data.

The fourth and last CIM correlate is Continuous Improvement of Quality.

CORRELATE 4:
CONTINUOUS IMPROVEMENT OF QUALITY

1. Learn and use QPC Tools.

2. Organize Management Team to focus on customer needs, identify vital few quality opportunities, and monitor system using quality assurance plan and system planning.

3. Use lead management principles of reality therapy and constructive feedback for special cause solutions.

4. Charter teams for solving the vital few quality opportunities.

5. Use plan-do-check/study-act to continuously improve for quality:

   a. TAPS model

   b. Design model

6. Form self-directed teams for continuous improvement of quality.

MANAGEMENT PRINCIPLES USED

ORGANIZING
Management team recognizes quality opportunities that will improve quality for the customers.

PLANNING
Use plan-do-check/study-act to solve problems.

CONTROLLING
1. Monitoring processes
2. Surveying customer needs
3. Performance goal index of product or service
4. Organizational health profiles
5. Supplier ratings and requirements

LEADING
Use facilitating skills and QPC tools.

CHAPTER 8

System Planning for Quality

Two hiking groups embarked from the same camp on separate daylong expeditions in an isolated wilderness area that none of the members had visited. The first group stopped for a moment upon taking the trail and made a careful survey of familiar landmarks. The second group, rushed because their breakfast eggs burned, hurriedly fled down the trail an hour later without taking note of their surroundings. Both groups became lost during the day, and each spent the remainder of the daylight and evening hours attempting to solve the problem of finding their way back to camp. And both succeeded. But there was one crucial difference: The early group spent only the afternoon, being guided back before dusk by the landmarks that had previously been identified, while the late bunch wandered aimlessly, well into the evening, taking guesses and hoping to find their way back to camp by what they came to realize was dumb luck.

In this analogy, both groups spent most of their day problem-solving rather than planning, in their attempts to return to camp. The early group's greater success in being the first back can be largely attributed to the foundation it laid by establishing landmarks with which to direct its actions. Planning accomplishes much the same purpose, enabling an organization to move into the future guided by pre-established landmarks to which it can return time and time again with relative ease.

Campus (or system) planning is an appropriate task for a steering committee such as the one established at Trail's End Middle School. The goal is nothing less than the transformation of the system into a CIM process. There are many good models for planning; this model will use the Four Correlates of Quality Schools as a foundation. Trail's End's system builds on the correlates, translating them into action points in order to make the transformation to a quality school.

To broaden input to develop a system plan for quality, the steering committee should involve a staff advisory committee, and an advisory committee of parents and community members. The parent/community advisory committee should be composed of persons interested in CIM or who use CIM principles in their jobs.

The System Planning for Quality model includes the following steps:

1. Analyze Mission Statement

  a. Use Six Hats tool:

    (1) Red Hat: Feeling and opinions about the school's mission

    (2) White Hat: What the school has done to fulfill the mission

    (3) Yellow Hat: The strengths of the system and environment to accomplish the mission

    (4) Black Hat: Obstacles to fulfilling the mission in the system and environment

    (5) Green Hat: Characteristics of an ideal Quality School

    (6) Blue Hat: Select the top three most important items in each hat.

  b. Review and understand knowledge base for accomplishing mission:

    (1) Four Quality Correlates

    (2) Deming literature

    (3) Juran literature

    (4) Glasser literature

    (5) Other CIM resources

2. Select Quality Initiatives:

  a. Use fishbone diagram with Four Quality Correlates as the effect. Brainstorm initiatives for achieving each correlate. The categories can be determined by the planners, but some starters are:

    (1) Work on the System:

      (a) Suppliers

        (b) Customers

        (c) Structure

        (d) Training

    (2) Adopt lead management principles:

        (a) Eliminate barriers and coercion.

        (b) The system

        (c) Training

        (d) In the classroom

    (3) Assess own quality:

        (a) Quality assurance

        (b) The system

        (c) In the classroom

        (d) Training

    (4) Continuous improvement:

        (a) Teams

        (b) The system

        (c) In the classroom

        (d) Training

3. Achieve consensus on Quality Initiatives:

    a. Use 5–3–1 Consensus tool.

    b. Decide on consensus percentage.

4. Place Quality Initiatives in annual phases.

5. Develop action plan for each phase:

    a. Develop strategies.

    b. Determine who will do what, when and where.

6. Decide on vital few customer problems to study for the year:

    a. Study Quality Assurance Plan.

    b. Decide on critical defects, excessive variance, customer dissatisfaction, excessive costs, and waste. Reach consensus on tackling from one to three of these quality opportunities.

    c. Use cause–effect diagrams to brainstorm causes with critical quality opportunities as effects.

    d. Reach consensus on vital few problems related to quality opportunities.

    e. Develop Pareto diagram to test consensus.

The steering committee should begin the planning session by analyzing the mission statement. This presents a good opportunity to review and affirm the beliefs of the committee members and staff. The mission statement should be revised at this juncture if beliefs have changed. The advisory committees should be included in this process, either separately or together with the steering group. The groups may want to use the Six Hats to clarify issues, then come up with the three most important items in each hat list. If the advisory committees do the Six Hats separately, their list should be considered in selecting the top three.

Before attempting to produce a plan, the school committees should have already completed training in the Four Quality Correlates. It helps if the parents, community, and students all are included in the training. Before launching into an action plan, steering committee members should study how Deming's Fourteen Points (Addendum) relate to public education.

COMMITMENT FOR CHANGE

Gaining commitment of management is perhaps the most difficult step. It certainly is the most important, since real change will not occur unless it gains the blessing and active participation of those on top of the personnel charts. A typical procedure by which management digests and embraces the new philosophy is:

1. **Top management will struggle over each of Deming's points and the principles of lead management.** They will agree on their meaning, and on the direction to take regarding them. They will agree to carry out the new philosophy.

2. **Top management must feel pain and dissatisfaction with past performance, and have courage to change. They must break out of line, even to the point of exile among their peers.** There must be a burning desire to transform the existing style of management.

3. **Top management will explain through meetings with employees why changes are necessary and why the current system will not produce quality.** A critical mass of supporters of change must arise from the meetings to support management's efforts to transform the organization. This critical mass of employees must understand the Fourteen Points and the Principles of Quality Schools.

4. Management must communicate to employees that every activity is a process that can be improved through teamwork.

QUALITY INITIATIVES

The Quality Initiatives are the basics of the System Plan for Quality. An initiative is a statement of what could be done to help achieve the Four Quality Correlates that would accomplish the mission of the school. Examples of quality initiatives are: "Establish a means for system planning for quality to be reviewed and revised each year" and "Teach control theory and reality therapy to the students."

The use of a fishbone diagram will help obtain possible initiatives via brainstorming. The categories help pinpoint areas for initiatives, and the effect guides the brainstorming to a common focus. An example of a fishbone diagram derived from a session is displayed here.

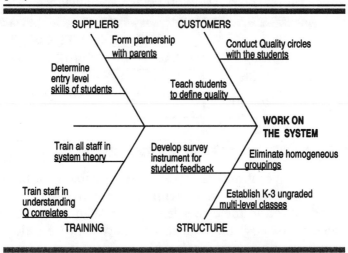

To reach consensus, the fishbone initiatives should be listed by quality correlate and similar initiatives combined. Be sure to include initiatives developed by the advisory committees. A final list of the initiatives should be prepared for steering committee members. The members should use the 5–3–1 consensus tool for establishing consensus. Ninety percent may be a good level of the ratings for consensus.

Once the priority initiatives have been selected, phases for implementation should be developed. A five-year phase period usually is appropriate. Selecting which initiatives to place in which phase is not an easy task: Each initiative must provide a foundation for a more ambitious initiative in future years of the plan. The effect of quality transformation is cumulative, like a snowball gathering girth and weight as it is rolled. Cost factors must be weighed; expensive changes should be phased in wherever possible, to avoid budget shock. However, the cost of most quality initiatives is minimal as compared with the amount saved by increasing efficiency. Difficult initiatives should be separated into phases because they require more time to implement. Time will be a very valuable commodity in the pursuit of quality.

Two tools that will help determine sequence, cost groupings, and difficulty are a process flow diagram and a difficulty/cost grid. The grid provides a visual picture of the priorities established by a group. Draw the following chart on butcher paper measuring at least 2' x 2'. Write each initiative on a Post-It™ note that can be placed in the appropriate category, depending on perceived cost and degree of difficulty.

		DEGREE OF DIFFICULTY		
		EASY	MODERATE	DIFFICULT
	HIGH			
COSTS	MEDIUM			
	LOW			

For example, if an initiative is easy to implement but bears a high cost, the sticky note with the initiative written on it should be placed in the upper left square. With this information the stickers can now be used to construct a process flow diagram showing the proper sequence.

Beginning with Quality Correlate 1, place the initiatives on a poster board in a PFD fashion. The correlates are not entirely sequential, but any change can be made after viewing the completed PFD. This will give the proper sequence of the initiatives.

As the PFD is developed, attention should be given to placing difficult initiatives with moderate or easy-to-implement initiatives. Also, high cost initiatives should be paired with low or medium cost initiatives. The last decision in this stage that the steering committee needs to make is where to draw the line separating the phases.

Once initiatives are grouped into phases, the first-year action plan must be developed. The steering committee should use a similar form for making decisions for implementing the initiatives.

ACTION PLAN

Strategies	Who Is Responsible?	Who Is Involved?	Begin Date	End Date	Where Performed
1.					
2.					
3.					
4.					
5.					

The action plan may be a function of the steering committee, or of a team chartered to implement the initiative.

The steering committee also should develop a performance goal index for measuring the success of the implementation phase. Indicator criteria for each initiative should be brainstormed. An example of a measurable indicator criteria for the initiative to teach students control theory and reality therapy is "The number of students taught the principles." The index should be reviewed at the end of the school year to determine if the next phase needs to address the initiative. The performance goal index should be reviewed each year to make sure the initiative is not forgotten.

Finally, the steering committee should create a Pareto diagram to isolate the vital few problems for the year, as explained in Chapter 6. It should now be included in the yearly system planning for quality. With a quality assurance plan in effect, the steering committee can focus on customer problems. The vital few problems will allow the steering committee to concentrate its energies on the critical problems confronting the organization regarding customer service and products—particularly student learning.

Each year the organization should devote time to system planning by reviewing the phases and gaining consensus on the vital few problems. The steps of system planning should be used annually to create a new phase and a new action plan. A new vital few should be agreed upon to guide the school's problem-solving focus during the year.

PRINCIPAL PAT ANN HOLD

Pat and the steering committee appointed two advisory committees to supplement the staff advisory committee, in an attempt to broaden input for the System Plan for Quality. One advisory committee was composed of fifteen parents and community members, four of whom had prior experience with CIM. The second advisory committee was composed of students from each grade level. Pat decided to take the steering committee off campus on a Friday for the first planning session. The members agreed to meet the next week, on a Saturday. Subsequent meetings would be on early-release days.

Pat gave each steering committee member a copy of the Four Campus Quality Correlates and the Four Classroom Quality Correlates, which had been developed by the subcommittee on continuous improvement goals.

FOUR CAMPUS QUALITY CORRELATES

CORRELATE 1: WORK ON THE SYSTEM

Understand your system and discuss quality with everyone in the system.

1. Know and understand what processes you own.
2. Understand who your internal and external customers are for each process, and discover the needs they have from each process.
3. Understand who your internal and external suppliers are, and enter into mutual beneficiary partnerships that improve the input to your process.
4. With the ideal school or classroom in mind, develop a purpose and a mission to improve the processes that meet customer needs.
5. Discuss quality in all places and at all times with managers, workers, customers, and suppliers.
6. Train and educate everyone in the system.

Make structural changes that fulfill the mission, satisfy the customer, and remove barriers to quality.

CORRELATE 2: ADOPT LEAD MANAGEMENT PRINCIPLES

1. Build trust.
2. Provide and promote a caring, enjoyable, risk-free climate within the school.
3. Eliminate fear by removing coercion as a means of motivating others (This means reducing the reliance on grades, rankings, summative tests, and subjective evaluations, as inspection tools.)
4. Break down barriers to cooperative efforts and continuous improvement for quality.
5. Ask workers and students for their input into decisions affecting them.
6. Facilitate and coach others to adopt lead management principles.
7. Collect data from all parts of the system (input, processes, and output) in order to base evaluations and decisions on data, not on opinions.
8. Provide training and education for all in lead management principles, control theory, and reality therapy.

CORRELATE 3: ASSESS OWN QUALITY

1. Understand process variation and use SPC tools for measuring defects.
2. Eliminate performance evaluations and merit pay based on performance.
3. Measure input of suppliers for quality.
4. Reduce reliance on grades as indicator of student mastery of learning.
5. Allow all workers to assess and improve their own processes:
   a. Delegate authority.
   b. Provide information and support.
   c. Develop trust in the organization.
   d. Train workers in SPC Tools.
6. Management should organize and plan for monitoring the system:
   a. Check sheets
   b. Control charts

    c. Histograms

    d. Performance index

    e. Organizational Health Survey

    f. Survey information

  7. Promote Strategic or System planning.

CORRELATE 4: CONTINUOUS IMPROVEMENT OF QUALITY

  1. Learn and use QPC Tools.

  2. Organize Management Team to focus on customer needs, identify vital few quality opportunities, and monitor system using quality assurance plan and system planning.

  3. Use lead management principles of reality therapy and constructive feedback for special cause solutions.

  4. Charter teams for solving the vital few quality opportunities.

  5. Use plan-do-check/study-act to continuously improve for quality:

    a. TAPS model

    b. Design model

  6. Form self-directed teams for continuous improvement of quality.

FOUR CLASSROOM QUALITY CORRELATES

CORRELATE 1: WORK ON THE SYSTEM

Discussion of quality with students and parents:

  1. Defining quality:

    a. Quality things in their lives

    b. Quality people in their lives

    c. Quality work and assignments

  2. Quality circles:

    a. Open-ended

    b. Diagnostic

    c. Problem-solving

  3. Develop with students a classroom Mission Statement:

    a. Work with students to develop student goals.

  4. Form a partnership with the parents.

Change the instruction in the class to action learning activities that involve all students and all learning styles.

CORRELATE 2: ADOPT LEAD MANAGEMENT PRINCIPLES

1. Obtain feedback from students on their needs and expectations, how they learn best, and what to them is important learning.
2. Teach students control theory principles.
3. Teach students Four Correlates of Quality.
4. Teach students how to use reality therapy for peer counseling.
5. Develop need-satisfying classrooms.
6. Use students for peer tutoring and peer counseling, and as teacher assistants.

CORRELATE 3: ASSESS OWN QUALITY

1. Develop criteria for quality assignment.
2. Rate assignments for quality.
3. Rate own assignment for quality.
4. Assess own homework grade.
5. Assess own project grade.
6. Allow students to design evaluation of learning
7. Develop means for student demonstration of mastery by asking students to show how they did it, explain questions on how, ask for self-assessment, agree on improvement needed, and repeat the cycle once improvement is completed.
8. Develop grading system based on mastery.
9. Focus on teaching students how to learn by:
   a. Eliminating memorization of facts
   b. Conducting open-book tests
   c. Cooperative learning activities

CORRELATE 4: CONTINUOUS IMPROVEMENT OF QUALITY

1. Allow students to continuously improve their grade for quality.
2. Teach students to use QPC tools.
3. Stop "averaging of grades" for sequential learning.
4. Promote continuous improvement of quality by allowing students to rework assignments at home.

5. Teach students problem-solving methods.

6. Teach content through use of problem-solving units.

Pat facilitated as the steering committee worked through the System Planning steps. The labor was long and hard, but the committee believed it was on the right track and, for once, had found direction in its efforts to improve. After several sessions of work, the steering committee produced a five-year phase plan for CIM. The plan was presented to the advisory committees for their approval; the yearly phases were presented to the faculty with explanations. Pat assured the staff that all members would get a chance to participate on a team to implement the action plan.

At the top of the list for the first year was training all employees in the Quality Correlates and underlying principles. The steering committee combined efforts with the staff advisory group to develop an action plan for training all personnel. By this time, the staff advisory committee had doubled in size as faculty members became interested in providing input. The explorers and scouts were using innovative techniques that other teachers noticed and discussed. Interest in trying something new was running high. Will had encouraged his peers to use some of the ideas he had developed in the classroom, and his students had spread the word to other teachers through their enthusiasm about what was happening in his class.

With a road map in place for the journey to CIM, Pat began to see the need for a management team to perform many of the functions of the old steering committee. She proposed to the steering committee that a management team be created, with herself as a member. The team would select a chairperson who would be responsible for working with the principal in developing an agenda. The management team would be responsible for the budget, personnel allocations and assignments, structural changes in the curriculum and courses, quality assurance planning and monitoring, organizational health analyzing and action planning, system planning for quality with action planning, training, determining the vital few quality opportunities, chartering teams, and celebrating successes.

The team members needed to become highly organized, so they appointed members to roles as recorder, summarizer, consensus checker, and meeting organizer. The recorder would publish the minutes of each meeting for the staff. At the end of each meeting, the summarizer would sum up the decisions made by the management team. The consensus checker was to be responsible for ascertaining that agreement was reached on decisions. The meeting organizer was responsible for setting up the meeting room and ensuring that needed equipment and supplies were available. The management team appointed two subteams, one for quality assurance and one for action planning. The quality assurance team was responsible for collecting data required by the quality assurance plan, and making it available to the management team. The team was also responsible for recommending teams or individuals for recognition at celebrations of success. The action planning team was charged with developing such plans for the current-phase initiatives. The team was also responsible for developing an action plan for improving the organizational health of the campus.

After the first year of staff training, Pat intended to dissolve the staff advisory committee, which had served its purpose of encouraging experimentation by risk-taking staff members. But it was now time to involve the entire staff. The parent advisory and student advisory committees would continue to operate, providing valuable input to both the management team and Pat. All management team decisions would be presented to the advisory committees for their recommendations. Too, breakthrough teams would be chartered to study the vital few quality opportunities developed by the management team. Pat knew it was important to involve as many staff members as possible in chartered teams.

Pat's role would be to help develop the agenda for management team meetings, take care of the day-by-day management of the school, and collect customer satisfaction data (to be sure the focus remained on the customer and not on the team members). Her role as advisor would be to influence the team to pay attention to its mission and put the customers first. As a fully converted lead manager, Pat felt comfortable with her new role, and chuckled to herself as she recalled how threatened she would have been a year before, had she been asked to cede decision-making to a team.

TEACHER WILL E. SURVIVE

Most of Trail's End's teachers sought eagerly to bend Will's ear about new classroom techniques they were trying. He in turn shared with them the exciting things taking place that were making learning more relevant. Will's classroom had evolved a system whereby students demonstrated mastery of a concept by showing how they did it, answering questions from their peers and Will, and then self-assessing their own learning. Homework had become solely a means to improve work until it was quality in the students' eyes. Will's students began to show remarkable self-direction, this culminating in the development of a community problem-solving unit. Using the design approach to problem-solving, the students developed a method for recycling paper in the school and at area businesses. Will was impressed by the manner in which the students planned the program with data they had collected. The students sampled community members on the need for recycling, then developed the features of what the product would be when delivered to a recycling plant. They created a process flow diagram showing how the paper would be collected and processed. The students used the QPC tools to arrive at consensus when decisions were made, then piloted the program at the school administration office for two weeks. Refinements were made in the process from data collected at certain stages. The students presented their plans to the management team for implementation in the school. The management team then recommended just that, for the campus. The students later met with the city council, and presented the plan with their data. The council shortly agreed to consider its use by the city.

For once, Will did not want the school year to end. Could he duplicate this experience next year? He knew that his adoption of the Classroom Quality Correlates over the last two years was a hit-or-miss proposition rather than a planned occurrence. Nonetheless, the result had been useful and enjoyable learning, at least for most of the students. (Most had earned an A or B.) He almost had to apologize to other teachers when they saw his grade distribution; some were still hooked on the bell-shaped curve for learning. His only problem was that he had not covered all the material—but he reminded himself that covering the material really wasn't the objective. That was helping students to learn how to learn.

Will gave each student a questionnaire that would measure both the climate for learning, and attitude toward learning, in the classroom. The data would be shown as bar graphs for future benchmarking.

WILL'S CLASS QUESTIONNAIRE

On a scale of 1–5, rate the following experiences or needs related to this classroom over this year.

	Strongly Disagree	Disagree	Not Sure	Agree	Strongly Agree
1. I had a feeling of success.	1	2	3	4	5
2. I felt I had ownership in class decisions.	1	2	3	4	5
3. The learning was fun.	1	2	3	4	5
4. The learning was useful.	1	2	3	4	5
5. There were choices involved in learning.	1	2	3	4	5
6. I strived for quality in my work.	1	2	3	4	5
7. I was willing to take risks in class.	1	2	3	4	5
8. I was able to assess my own work.	1	2	3	4	5
9. I was able to continuously improve work.	1	2	3	4	5
10. Overall, I enjoyed the class.	1	2	3	4	5

Comments: _____

_____

_____

What would you change that could improve learning in the classroom for all students?

_____

WILL'S WIFE, WANNA

Will's wife, Wanna, was an elementary school teacher. After a year of listening to Will discuss how he used CIM in the classroom, she decided to get her feet wet by giving it a try. She started gently by having the students make individual mobiles portraying items representing quality in their lives. On a writing assignment, she asked students to brainstorm with her on what constitutes a quality paper. She displayed ten samples from the previous year. The students then reached consensus on the criteria for quality writing. Wanna thereafter asked the students to assess the ten sample papers for quality, according to the criteria they had selected. On their next writing assignment, she asked them to put a Q on the paper if they thought it was quality. After the assignments were completed, she conducted her first quality circle meeting on the topic, "How do I know if my paper is quality?" She explored with the students why they had or had not put a Q on their papers. Wanna ended the unit by telling the students she was going to keep individual folders in class in which students could place quality work.

Wanna worked hard for the remainder of the year to create a class which all students had a sense of worth, a feeling of belonging, and the understanding that the teacher really cared about them. She continued to allow students to assess their own work. She graded the work and averaged her grade with their grade, always asking the students to explain why they rated their papers as they did.

Homework assignments became activities that involved parents, rather than monotonous work sheets. She required the students to watch educational programs on television for discussion the next day. None of the homework was graded. She began allowing students to improve their grade by taking completed work back home and redoing it. A few students avidly took advantage of this innovation, and their learning appeared to increase as their interest in reworking papers soared.

By midyear the quality of work had improved so that grades were not necessary as a daily inspection device. She regularly conducted quality circle meetings using open-ended, educational diagnostic and problem-solving topics. She conducted one on grades and another on what "makes" a good substitute. The students decided that the teacher could interview them to determine if their work was quality. They would show the teacher how they could do the work, answer questions from the teacher, and then self-assess their work for quality. The student and teacher would talk about possible ways to improve the work. If the student chose to improve it, then the cycle would repeat when the student was ready. This required Wanna to constantly walk around the class, coaching the students. She formed cooperative learning teams for many assignments, saving time because she could ask the group to demonstrate how they did the assignment. She would ask different students in the group to explain how they arrived at their solutions. Later, she appointed two students to help check work for mastery, after showing them how.

Wanna believed that reading skills were the true test of quality in elementary school. So many students' self-concepts were shattered when they were not able to learn to read as fast as their peers. These students usually became discouraged and, years later, dropped out of Trail's End Middle School. After studying the Quality School Correlates, Wanna shelved the basal readers and began using literature that students enjoyed. If what they read was neither enjoyable nor relevant, role-oriented students would never learn to read successfully, Wanna believed. She used newspapers, cartoons, comic books, novels, and stories brainstormed by the class. The students read to each other, to their parents, and to her. The only way to learn to read is to read, Wanna thought, so she read to the students stories they liked. No worksheets were used. The students had to demonstrate that they understood what they read by role-playing, acting out a book, or telling another student or teacher about it.

During the last half of the year, Wanna used the TAPS model for problem-solving units, with the students working in teams. Grades were no longer given, except at report-card time. Students kept their own charts of their work, noting a Q for quality or an M for mastery. The teacher checked each student's quality folder periodically for improvement. Wanna was pleased with the progress she had made in building on the quality concepts she knew. She began planning for the next year, when she would systematically introduce the four correlates into the classroom from Day One.

SYSTEM FEEDBACK

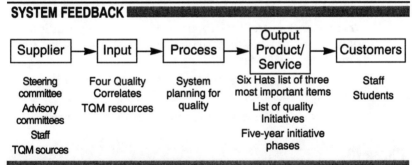

Supplier	Input	Process	Output Product/Service	Customers
Steering committee	Four Quality Correlates	System planning for quality	Six Hats list of three most important items	Staff
Advisory committees	TQM resources		List of quality Initiatives	Students
Staff			Five-year initiative phases	
TQM sources				

THE DICKINSON EXPERIENCE

Dickinson Independent School District administrators spent the first year examining CIM, using the Four Quality Correlates as a guide. During the summer all administrators participated in System Planning for Quality. The product was a five-year phase-in of quality initiatives. That plan is presented here as a guide for those planning a districtwide move to quality.

Phase I

1. All campus and departmental personnel are trained in the Quality School Approach, which includes the Four Quality School Correlates: (1) Work on the System; (2) Adopt Lead Management Principles; (3) Assess Own Quality; and (4) Continuous Improvement for Quality.

2. The districtwide Management Team and the Student Success Team are solving the vital few problems of the district using District Quality Breakthrough Teams.

3. The campus staff has read *The Quality School,* and discussed questions relating to the book.

4. Campuses and departments are organized in the Quality Improvement Process, with a Management Team chartering Quality Breakthrough Teams (QBT).

Phase II

1. All campuses and departments are involved in System Planning for Quality. The product is a list of quality initiatives for the current year, and action plans for each initiative.

2. Control charts are commonly used by all administrators.

3. A District Quality Assurance Plan is developed and implemented.

4. A communication process is in place for internal suppliers and customers to provide input, expectations, and satisfaction/dissatisfaction. Customer/supplier meetings are common.

5. All school staff have received training in control theory and reality therapy.

6. New personnel are trained in the Four Quality Correlates.

Phase III

1. Students in grades 5–12 are assessing their own quality, for continuous improvement.

2. Students in grades K–12 are involved in class discussions relating to quality work.

3. A partnership with parents (suppliers) and the schools is established with school expectations, self-assessment by parents, and school assessment of expectations met all in place.

4. All managers (administrators, leaders, and teachers) are using the principles of lead management.

5. Mastery of need-to-know curriculum and student exit outcomes are measured and charted. Changes are made by those closest to the process, by using the plan, do, check/study-act cycle in TAPS teams.

Phase IV

1. Students in grades K–12 are taught the scientific method for problem-solving (TAPS model) and use of quality process control tools.

2. All major external suppliers are evaluated for quality, and expectations documented.

3. Charters are accepted for volunteer employee TAPS teams.

4. Students in grades K–12 are taught components of control theory and reality therapy.

5. Staff members are evaluating their own work for quality.

6. Training and retraining is ongoing.

Phase V

1. The campus staff is implementing the Four Classroom Quality Correlates.

2. Control charts are commonly used by all TAPS teams.

3. At least 75 percent of the teachers and support personnel are involved in TAPS teams, thereby improving their processes.

4. The quality of the district has improved considerably, as evidenced by:

    a. Reduction in dropouts and at-risk students

    b. Increase in student promotions and graduates

    c. Increase in standardized test scores

    d. Increase in number of students in advanced classes

    e. Reduction in remedial programs and special at-risk programs

    f. External and internal customer satisfaction with school product

    g. Decrease in injury claims and accidents

    h. OHI profiles indicating quality health in all organizations

    i. Increase in mastery of reading and math

    j. Internal customer satisfaction in Maintenance, Transportation, Child Nutrition Services, and Special Services

    k. Decrease in number of students labeled

    l. Increase in quality of student work as evidenced by:

      (1) Grades

      (2) Achievement scores

      (3) Surveys of students and parents

      (4) Quality of student portfolios

    m. Increase in attendance by all personnel and students

    n. Decrease in discipline problems in school and on buses

    o. Maintenance of both facilities and vehicles rated quality

    p. Follow-up studies of graduates indicate graduates successful

    q. Increase in involvement in extracurricular activities

5. Train and retrain.

Phase VI

Continuously improve the processes implemented, and continue to train/retrain.

The first-year quality initiatives were assigned to break-through teams (or management teams) for development of action plans for implementation. Over a period of two years, each department and campus responded to its quality plans by developing customer-driven innovations with a customer focus. These plans included changing the names of the departments and buildings to reflect customer service, interdisciplinary teaming in secondary grades, prekindergarten programs, full-day kindergarten, multiage classes, block scheduling, and other organizational improvements.

EVOLUTION OF THE MANAGEMENT TEAM

Once planning and training have been organized, the steering committee should evolve into a management team, which will meet the requirements of site-based decision-making needed to eventually empower the workers. The campus and department management teams in Dickinson were delegated all personnel responsibilities and personnel funds. All decisions not affecting other departments/campuses, district policy, or costs beyond their budget, could be approved by the management team without seeking approval from upper management. Effective two-way communication is essential in this stage, or changes will occur at the sites without the knowledge of the central administrators and Board of Trustees. Periodic reviews and examination of management-team minutes will help prevent surprises. Involvement of the parent advisory committee in management-team decisions will prevent decisions from being circumvented by the board due to political pressure. Providing the board with management-team minutes is a good way to keep them informed. The plan for site-based decision-making in Dickinson was developed during several lengthy negotiations between central and campus administrators. The Dickinson site-based plan is detailed below.

STAFF INVOLVEMENT IN DECISION-MAKING

DECISIONS	CAMPUS/DEPT. OR DISTRICT	WHO RECOMMENDS	WHO HAS FINAL DECISION
1. Preparation of budget	Campus/Department	TAPS Teams	Management Team
	District	Assistant Superintendents	Management Action Team to Administrative Board to School Board
2. System Planning	Campus/ Department	Management Team	Management Team
	District	Administrative Board	Management Action Team to Administrative Board to School Board
3. New Programs	Campus/Department	TAPS Teams	Management Team
	District	Management Action Team and Student Success Team	Administrative Board to School Board
4. Selection of Campus/Dept. Equipment	Campus/Department	TAPS Teams	Management Team
5. Organizational Health Action Plan	Campus/Department Team	Management Team	Management Team
	District	Management Action Team	Administrative Board

DECISIONS	CAMPUS/DEPT. OR DISTRICT	WHO RECOMMENDS	WHO HAS FINAL DECISION
6. Instructional materials	Campus/Department	TAPS Teams	TAPS Teams
7. Instructional methodology	Campus/Department	TAPS Teams	TAPS Teams
8. Curriculum	Campus/Department	TAPS Teams	TAPS Teams
	District	Student-Success Team and Teacher Advisory Committee	Administrative Board to School Board
9. Employee Welfare Concerns	Campus/Department	Staff and Management Team	Principal
	District	Personnel Services Committee	Superintendent
10. Staff Development	Campus/Department	TAPS Teams and Management Team	Management Team
	District	Student Success Team and Teacher Advisory Committee	Administrative Board
11. Facility Additions	District	Principals/Directors	Superintendent
12. Personnel Allocations	Campus/Department	Principal and Management Team	Superintendent and Board
13. Policy	Campus/Department	TAPS Teams and Management Team	Management Team
	District	Management Action Team	Administrative Board to School Board
14. Technology	District	Student Success Team	Administrative Board to School Board
15. Hiring of Staff	Campus/Department	TAPS Teams, Management Team, and Principal	Personnel Director to Superintendent to School Board
	District	Individual Departments	Superintendent to School Board

The operation of the Dickinson School District was entrusted to two teams: The District Management Action Team, and the District Student Success Team. The Management Action Team was composed of support directors and several principals. Subteams working under the Management Action Team were the Quality Assurance Team and the Action Planning Team. The Student Success Team was composed of all curriculum management personnel and several principals. The principals rotated each year between the two teams, while the others remained on the same team. The Student Success Team maintained the same two subteams. The Quality Assurance Team was responsible for collecting the data required in the quality assurance plan for the district. It was responsible for the district performance goal index data. Periodically, the team would report to the parent team a summary of the data collected, and any other data required on request. The team was responsible for recognizing breakthrough team successes and celebrating them. A budget was provided for these activities. The Action Planning Team was responsible for action planning for quality initiatives, organizational health action plans, and any other action planning required. The team was also responsible for replying to Idea Card suggestions from employees. Action was taken on the ideas worth pursuing, and recognition was given to those whose ideas had merit. The superintendent was a member of both the Management Action Team and the Student Success Team, but was not the chairperson (who usually was an assistant superintendent). The organizational plan and responsibilities are displayed in the flow diagram on the page 156.

MANAGEMENT PRINCIPLES USED

ORGANIZING

The steering committee is transformed into a management team.

PLANNING

System Planning for Quality is instituted by the steering committee.

CONTROLLING

A performance goal index is developed for assessing progress in the implementation of the System Plan.

LEADING

The manager moves to a coaching and facilitating mode in order to empower management teams to make decisions to accomplish the mission of the school.

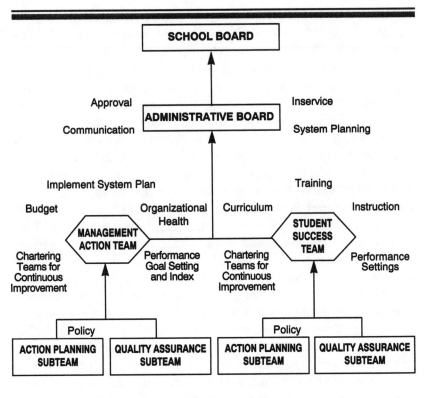

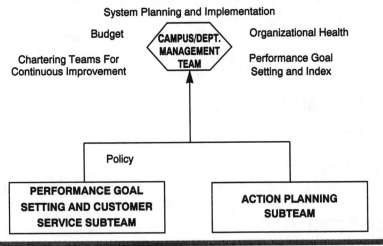

Training and Education

Deming's Sixth Point is, "Institute training and retraining." At seminars across the nation, the patriarch of the quality movement said, "Train everybody. And I mean everybody." Without training, CIM is only a dream. Many companies involved in CIM require fifty to 100 clock-hours of training per year, per employee. School districts that are following CIM principles are beginning to restructure their stodgy staff-development functions to fit the demands of a work force that never can learn enough. As we move past the Industrial Age into the Information Age, training becomes the means to the end of quality.

But how does a school approach CIM training after years of the status quo? The plan-do-check/study-act cycle is appropriate for planning effective training as well as continuous improvement. First, the management team needs a plan for the training, always remembering to try it first on a small scale and following up with evaluation. When the training design and modules are field-tested, and meet a standard for quality, then do it: Train all appropriate personnel. Since CIM is a fundamental rethink of processes, the new knowledge that employees need is often applicable to all categories, from teachers to food servers.

The management team should treat the quality opportunity of providing training for everyone as a design problem. The product of a design model is a list of training modules needed, the content of each module, and a plan of how to deliver the training. The plan will unfold as teams work through the eight steps for product design:

1. **Collect internal and external customer needs.**

   Needs:

   Work on the System, Adopt Lead Management, Assess Own Quality, and Continuous Improvement of Quality

2. **Develop criteria for design.**

Goals and Criteria:

GOAL—WORK ON THE SYSTEM

Criteria:

- Understand system theory.
- Know who your suppliers and customers are, internal and external.
- Understand your process.
- Understand the principles of Quality Improvement.

GOAL—ADOPT LEAD MANAGEMENT

Criteria:

- Understand the differences between lead management and boss management.
- Understand control theory and stimulus–response theory.
- Understand the principles of reality therapy.
- Understand how to coach and facilitate others.
- Understand empowerment.

GOAL—ASSESS OWN QUALITY

Criteria:

- Understand Statistical Process Control.
- Understand variation.
- Know why evaluations based on performance are counterproductive.
- Know how to measure supplier quality.
- Know what is need for workers to assess their own quality.
- Be able to use check sheets, control charts, histograms, and performance goal indexes.
- Know the differences between common and special causes.

GOAL—CONTINUOUS IMPROVEMENT OF QUALITY

Criteria:

- Be able to use Quality Process Control tools.
- Understand the TAPS Model for continuously improving process quality.
- Be able to recognize quality opportunities.
- Understand how to solve special cause problems and common cause problems.

3. Determine format, and develop product or service features.

Writing teams will design the actual contents of the modules to meet each set of criteria. For example, one module would be "Understand System Theory."

The module could be developed using the plan-do-check/study-act cycle to increase understanding. The format design is displayed below.

PLAN:

- Goal to accomplish:
- Module:
  - Focus
  - Content, concepts, and cooperative group activities
  - Dependent practice
  - Feedback and summarizing
  - Trainer guide

DO:

- Independent practice activities for the workplace

CHECK:

- Feedback on workplace practice
- Adjustments

ACT ON THE SYSTEM:

- Use in the workplace
- Monitoring and feedback
- Recognizing success

4. Develop a performance goal index.

Using the criteria, the team should develop a performance goal index to measure the effectiveness of the training modules. The criteria for the performance goal index are number of manhours of training per employee, rating of training by trainee, number of staff members seeking advance training, and evidence of use of training.

Once the training modules are developed, the team will design the process for delivering the training to the staff. A system process flow diagram showing the roles of the supplier (module writers), process owners (trainers), and customers (trainees) is a very useful tool for service designs. Notice the three roles and the features under those roles. Separate procedures can be developed for each role, once the flow diagram is completed.

When a plan for the introductory CIM training of all personnel is complete, similar design plans need to be developed for advanced training, general job training, and job-specific training. Each personnel classification should have a training plan specific to its needs, in addition to the generic CIM training.

Here is an example of advanced training using the Four Quality Correlates as guides.

QUALITY SCHOOL CORRELATE 1: WORK ON THE SYSTEM

1. System theory and satisfying the customer
2. Use of the Quality School Classroom Correlates

QUALITY SCHOOL CORRELATE 2: ADOPT LEAD MANAGEMENT PRINCIPLES

1. Control theory and reality therapy
2. Leadership training
3. Conducting meetings
4. Facilitator training
5. Cooperative learning
6. Noncoercive classroom management

QUALITY SCHOOL CORRELATE 3: ASSESS OWN QUALITY

1. SPC training
2. Performance indexing
3. Mastery learning
4. Authentic assessments and use of portfolios

QUALITY SCHOOL CORRELATE 4: CONTINUOUS IMPROVEMENT OF QUALITY

1. Teaching strategies and methodologies
2. Teaming skills
3. Curriculum mapping and outcome based education
4. Advance Team Approach to Problem Solving
5. Benchmarking techniques

Districts often turn to outside consultants to develop and present CIM training, but it is worth the time and effort for districts to develop their own modules. Employee buy-in to the concepts appears to be higher in districts where employees have developed and conducted their own training. Perhaps this is because the training is more relevant to a particular district when it is developed by its own employees. The training should be process-focused, meaning that participants need to discuss with peers the concepts presented. Only through discussion and disagreement will individual value systems be tested and possibly changed. Peer pressure is still the most influential factor in change; CIM training should be anything but dull lecture and presentations.

The trainers need to model coaching and facilitating skills. Coaching involves asking questions that lead one to improve the quality of work until the extra quality added is not worth the time spent. Questions that trainers should ask groups and individuals in dependent and independent practice are along these lines:

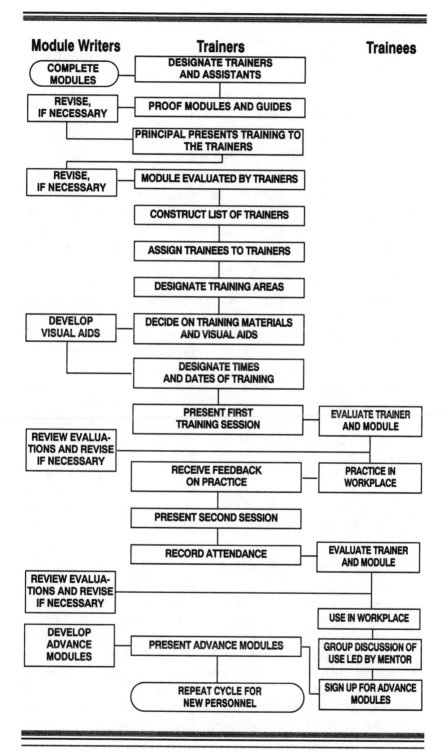

Module Writers	Trainers	Trainees
COMPLETE MODULES	DESIGNATE TRAINERS AND ASSISTANTS	
REVISE, IF NECESSARY	PROOF MODULES AND GUIDES	
	PRINCIPAL PRESENTS TRAINING TO THE TRAINERS	
REVISE, IF NECESSARY	MODULE EVALUATED BY TRAINERS	
	CONSTRUCT LIST OF TRAINERS	
	ASSIGN TRAINEES TO TRAINERS	
	DESIGNATE TRAINING AREAS	
DEVELOP VISUAL AIDS	DECIDE ON TRAINING MATERIALS AND VISUAL AIDS	
	DESIGNATE TIMES AND DATES OF TRAINING	
	PRESENT FIRST TRAINING SESSION	EVALUATE TRAINER AND MODULE
REVIEW EVALUATIONS AND REVISE IF NECESSARY	RECEIVE FEEDBACK ON PRACTICE	PRACTICE IN WORKPLACE
	PRESENT SECOND SESSION	
	RECORD ATTENDANCE	EVALUATE TRAINER AND MODULE
REVIEW EVALUATIONS AND REVISE IF NECESSARY		USE IN WORKPLACE
DEVELOP ADVANCE MODULES	PRESENT ADVANCE MODULES	GROUP DISCUSSION OF USE LED BY MENTOR
	REPEAT CYCLE FOR NEW PERSONNEL	SIGN UP FOR ADVANCE MODULES

- What you are doing? Show me.
- How did you do it?
- How would you use what you are doing in the workplace?
- Could you improve what you are doing? How?
- Could you do that in the time remaining, or take it home and improve it?
- What have you changed? How have you changed it?
- Do you think you can make it even better?
- What did you learn from doing this?

The role of the facilitator is to use the tools, which will work only if one takes the time to use them. Facilitators do not have the answers; their role is to help others to solve the problem. Trainers must model this role if they expect others to follow suit when it is their time.

Employees who are reluctant to try new things, or who are skeptical of the CIM concepts, may need an incentive to do the extra training each year needed for CIM. Training can be tied to pay as long as performance is not evaluated. Attendance should be the criteria. Those who are interested in presenting training should get credit in an incentive pay system for teaching courses. Most employees will discover that it is refreshing and rewarding to improve one's skills, and will seek more training when it is offered, regardless of the pay. Comp days are another way to get employees to take training. Employees can get a comp day during the school year for taking a day of training in the summer. It is also important to offer a wide range of training opportunities during the school year for those who aren't interested in coming back to school in the summer. And remember: Employees should be surveyed to determine which times and dates are most convenient for them.

PRINCIPAL PAT ANN HOLD

Pat was anxious to extend to the entire staff the training that the committees had received. She asked for, and got, several volunteers from the old steering and staff advisory committees to be trainers or module writers. Trainers selected assistants who had limited exposure to CIM concepts, but who wanted to learn by assisting them. The training group spent months planning the logistics of the training. The team of writers met independent of the trainers. The team of writers selected its own facilitator and chairperson, and began using the design model for preparing the modules, training guides, and flow chart of the process of delivering the training.

Pat had decided to include everyone in the training—building keepers, cafeteria workers, instructional aides, and secretaries. She even convinced some bus drivers who delivered students to the campus to participate. And she invited parents and community members to join the initial training. The trainer team recommended using early-release days and already scheduled inservice days for the initial 30 clock-hours of training. The training modules were:

Work on the System: 6 clock-hours

Adopt Lead Management Principles: 12 clock-hours

Assess own Quality: 6 clock-hours

Continuous Improvement of Quality: 6 clock-hours

In addition, the team set aside one hour per week for teachers to study and discuss, in a quality circle format, prepared questions from Mary Walton's *The Deming Management Method* and William Glasser's *The Quality School*. The Four Quality Correlates for the Classroom were the most challenging part of the discussions, as teachers pondered how to apply them in the classroom. Everyone knew it would be a challenging year for the staff.

Pat continued to remind herself that the key to CIM was becoming a lead manager. All the other correlates could be misconstrued or used coercively if Pat did not develop as that type of manager. To strengthen the school's lead management emphasis, a four-day module was prepared on advanced training in control theory, reality therapy, noncoercive classroom management, how to work with role- and goal-oriented students, conducting quality circles, coaching, and facilitating. The four days were scattered throughout the year, to allow participants to practice what they learned. Between sessions each participant paired up with a problem student so as to begin using reality therapy counseling. Teachers each were asked to conduct a quality circle meeting. They had to read one book on CIM, and keep a journal of how control theory was used in their daily lives. And they were encouraged to institute some of the noncoercive classroom management techniques. During each training session, lively discussions would focus on the experiences gained in the classroom.

The Management Team brainstormed future training needs for the campus. The training modules brainstormed by the team came under three categories: Just-in-Time Training (JIT), general job training, and job-specific training. JIT would be reserved for skills that were needed by newly formed teams, or immediate use in the workplace. Before a team could function properly, at least one of the members would need JIT facilitator training. All the members would have training in QPC tools, and use of the TAPS Model. Teams needing quality assurance tools would take training in control charts, histograms, check sheets, and performance goal indexing.

General job-training modules would include safety and CPR training, leadership styles, learning styles, product/service design planning, system planning, conducting meetings, team-building, and implementing classroom quality correlates. Job-specific training would be developed by each job classification, using design teams. The training would relate to specific skills needed in the workplace. Teachers would be offered training in cooperative learning, mastery learning, outcome-based education, classroom management, authentic assessments, and other strategies for the classroom. Secretaries would receive training in computer skills, filing, customer service, and other job-specific skills.

Writing teams would be chartered each year, to develop the modules. The management team struggled with how best to reimburse employees for their work, and how to get staff members to volunteer to teach the sessions. It wasn't easy, but the management team knew that CIM would fly only if the staff became well-educated in its use. Pat knew she was gambling that the staff would become enthusiastic about learning new ideas and also be willing to work on teams and teach the courses. Only the future would tell.

To keep focused on creating a quality organization, Pat asked several management team members to visit other schools using CIM each year. Pat selected four or five schools that had become leaders in restructuring. This kept the management team current on quality practices in the region. She also sent each member to at least a single quality-related workshop outside the district each year. This investment in training guaranteed that new ideas were introduced in brainstorming alternatives during problem-solving.

TEACHER WILL E. SURVIVE

Will soon became active as a trainer in the initial CIM sessions with all personnel. He had asked another teacher in his department to be his assistant, and found soon after that the teacher was starting to use CIM techniques in class. It helped that Pat was encouraging everyone to get "out of the box," meaning to break out of their mind-sets concerning how learning should occur.

Will continued to set goals with his students, and especially those with learning problems. He used the Shewhart cycle of plan-do-check/study-act as a model, working with the students to develop a plan for the year that would lead to successful learning. He used reality therapy techniques to help students create their plans. When the plan was free of defects, the student was ready to act on the system—that is, use it every day in the classroom.

During the last six weeks of school, Will allowed the classes to develop a quality unit on their own. He acted as an advisor and offered words of wisdom only when asked. The students developed visual presentations and an evaluation to determine if they had mastered the unit. The unit came off without a hitch by using cooperative groups, with student monitors in place of Will. He just sat back and watched—and grinned. While other teachers were fighting the battles of spring fever, summer anticipation, and boredom, Will had given control to the students, and they were handling it just fine, thank you. This had been a great year. He was ready to use system planning during the summer, to plan his class for the next year.

Will spent the last two weeks teaching the students about quality. He taught them control theory, lead management principles, and how to use reality therapy. While it was only an introduction, Will could tell that many students picked up on the ideas because they had seen them in practice in his class.

SYSTEM FEEDBACK

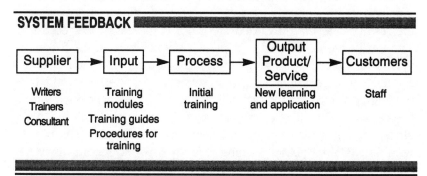

THE DICKINSON EXPERIENCE

The Dickinson Independent School District took Dr. Deming's advice to heart and literally trained everyone. All 720 employees received thirty clock-hours of CIM training, conducted in heterogeneous groups over the course of a year. The format was heavy on discussion and light on lecture, giving the employees ample time to debate concepts and give their opinions. Employees were grouped differently for each session so they could have different trainers and meet new people. The four quality correlates were used as guides for constructing the modules. All administrators served as trainers, including support directors and business office managers. Some had never taught, much less presented CIM to their peers, but all agreed it was a great experience. Each administrator selected an assistant (usually a teacher), but some assistants were bus drivers, cafeteria managers, or secretaries. In addition, all campuses conducted weekly study groups for a year, using Glasser's *The Quality School*. Questions were used to stimulate discussion of the concepts.

All classifications in the district formed teams to design their own training plans. The training plans for teachers, administrators, and secretaries were approved by the Student Success Team. The Management Action Team approved the training plans for all support services. To free up sufficient time for teacher training, the district added three days to teacher contracts, and secured a waiver from the state for five additional days in the regular school calendar. This supplied 56 clock-hours of training for teachers. However, this still wasn't enough, so the district developed a Quality Improvement Incentive Plan, to give personnel an incentive to train, to be involved in breakthrough teams, to teach classes, and to stay with the district. The plan awarded credit for completing selected items. The credits would convert to stipend amounts, paid in the following year. Training catalogs listing courses are distributed to all personnel for the summer, fall, and spring sessions. Personnel would take training approved for their specific training plan. A handbook would be available for each classification, containing the training plan, along with instructions for recording the credit. Each employee would maintain a yellow training card on which to record his or her clock-hours. Each year the employees would complete a survey of the clock-hours of training, membership on teams, clock-hours of teaching training courses, and other credit information. Total credits would be determined, and payroll would record the stipends earned for next year. An example of an incentive plan for bus drivers is listed below. (All other personnel have a similar plan.)

QUALITY IMPROVEMENT INCENTIVE PLAN FOR BUS DRIVERS

Stipulations for training

1. Maximum credit during 3-year period is 210 clock-hours or 13 credits. If you have a maximum of 210 clock hours, then you must maintain 30 clock hours of training every 3 years to keep the 13 credits.
2. Training must fit transportation's training plan approved by management action team and administrative team.
3. All bus drivers must complete 30 hours of continuous improvement training before one can receive any quality improvement incentive plan credit—these hours will not count as clock hours for credit proposes. Only hours after June 1, 1992 will count toward credit.
4. Training may be taken on school time for credit.

Experience

CREDIT ITEMS	CREDITS
Dickinson Experience In Current Position 1–3 Years	1
Dickinson Experience In Current Position 4–6 Years	1
Dickinson Experience In Current Position 7–10 Years	1
Dickinson Experience In Current Position 11+ Years	2
Total	**5**

Training Credit

CREDIT ITEMS		CREDITS
30–44	Clock-hours	1
45–59	Clock-hours	1
60–74	Clock-hours	1
75–89	Clock-hours	1
90–104	Clock-hours	1
105–119	Clock-hours	1
120–134	Clock-hours	1
135–149	Clock-hours	1
150–164	Clock-hours	1
165–179	Clock-hours	1
180–194	Clock-hours	1
195–209	Clock-hours	1
210+	Clock-hours	1
Total		**13**

Designated Training for Credit

CREDIT ITEMS	CREDITS
Certified as a facilitator—12 hours and practice	2
Certified in safety training management	2
Advanced CIM training	1
Total	**5**

(Certification will be determined by course content, practice, and demonstration)

Teaming

CREDIT ITEMS	CREDITS
Member of management team (1 each year. Maximum of 2 credits)	2
Member of TAPS Team on volunteer basis (must be a member each year or lose credit)	1
Served on a breakthrough team (1 each year, maximum of 3 credits—will lose 1 after 3 years if not on a breakthrough team)	3
Personnel service committee, employee-benefits committee, or sick-bank committee member (maximum 1 credit)	1
Facilitated A Team	2
Total	**9**

Presentations of Training (Every 3 years will lose 12 hours)

CREDIT ITEMS	CREDITS
6–12 Clock-hours	1
13–18 Clock-hours	1
19–24 Clock-hours	1
25–30 Clock-hours	1
31–36 Clock-hours	1
37–42 Clock-hours	1
43$^+$ Clock-hours	1
Total	**7**

Stipend Pay

CREDITS	STIPEND
0–4	0
5–8	$ 200
9–12	$ 350
18–16	$ 500
1–21	$ 650
22–26	$ 800
27–32	$ 950
33–38	$1100
39$^+$	$1250

(Bus drivers must serve 1 year in the district before becoming eligible for the Quality Improvement Incentive Plan)

MANAGEMENT PRINCIPLES USED

ORGANIZING

Training locations, class rolls, equipment, printing, materials, evaluation of training, assignment of trainers, writer teams, and trainer teams

PLANNING

Training plans and Quality Improvement Incentive Plans

CONTROLLING

Assessment of training and trainers

LEADING

Modeling lead management during training

Team Empowerment for Continuous Improvement

Empowerment gives employees the latitude to make decisions, within agreed parameters, that enable them to improve their processes and quality. Following the Four Quality Correlates to restructure the operations of a school district will produce top-down commitment with bottom-up empowerment. In this sense, Continuous Improvement Management goes beyond the site-based management systems now in place in many states. Site-based management typically mandates that certain decisions, formerly made at the central office, now must be made by a team of campus personnel. Unfortunately, in most states the education agency mandates a type of site-based management that does not guarantee that the quality of the decisions will be any better than in the "good old days" of central-office decision-making.

Empowerment, in any form, is both the immediate and the ultimate goal as systems move toward CIM. In the short term, individual empowerment will produce isolated pockets of quality processes in an organization. However, only through teaming will empowerment pay multiple dividends. Teams produce synergy, the effect caused when the sum of the parts is greater than the whole. The ability of the team when it is performing is greater than the sum of the individual abilities. Management teams, breakthrough teams, design teams, and other teams have been discussed in terms of the Four Quality Correlates. These teams have been formed either for organizational purposes or to solve a problem and then dissolve, but are not used for continuous improvement. Self-directed, voluntary teams will empower employees and improve quality constantly and lastingly. In industry these teams are called natural work groups, quality circles, process improvement teams, and other names that denote teams composed predominantly of process owners operating as a team to improve their own processes.

Only when the Four Quality Correlates are in place should a school begin forming self-directed teams. Management literature is replete with examples of attempts by U.S. companies to form, before the employees and management were ready, self-directed teams to improve quality. Most ended in failure. Teaming is one of the last components of CIM to be initiated; as a quality initiative it should be in Phase 4 or later. It may take three to four years for an organization to be at the readiness level for self-directed teams, since management must be ready to delegate almost complete authority over their processes to teams, if real improvement is to occur.

Managers who still are clinging to boss management will not be able to handle self-directed teams. There must be effective two-way communication for self-directed teams to flourish; boss managers typically do not seek the feedback necessary, or free up needed information, for self-directed teams to effectively operate. Eager they may be, but employees who work under a boss manager will only become more frustrated and fed up with the system if they try to implement self-directed teams where boss management prevails. Self-directed teams need data provided by the organization, data which are not likely to be readily available until a system quality assurance plan is in effect. Self-assessment of quality by individuals also needs to occur, and by then the training required to operate as a team should have been completed. Staff members should have had time to practice these new skills before applying them in self-directed teams. After three or four years of CIM, many if not most staff members will have participated in a breakthrough team, using the tools of a TAPS model or a design model. They will by then be familiar with control charts, check sheets, histograms, and performance goal indexes.

There are many barriers to effective customer service and quality improvement, ranging from defective raw material to poorly managed systems that lower worker morale and motivation. For the efficiency of the organization, management must be given time to remove as many of these barriers as possible before self-directed teams begin to operate. These barriers can become serious obstacles to self-directed teams that do not have sufficient authority to remove them. Many are barriers between departments that will actually undermine team solutions if left in place. For example, it would be very difficult to form self-directed teams in a secondary school wherein everything is organized around subject matter. Management should initiate the move to organizing around students, and then self-directed teams will become a natural progression. The focus of the team must be the customer, and not a product (such as math or English). This is not to say that the curriculum is not important—but that it is only one component of the process of instructing students. The curriculum will never be integrated with other curricula, so long as math teachers talk only to math teachers, or social studies teachers communicate only with each other. The self-directed team needs to be built around the process of the instruction of a common core of students. Then the communications will focus on how to improve instruction to these students, and not on how to create curricula that teachers enjoy teaching but students cannot learn.

Four ingredients must be present before a self-directed team can be formed. First, the manager, or management team, must have the means to provide useful information to the team. The self-directed team cannot operate without information traditionally reserved for top management. They must have budget information, costs of equipment and materials, control chart data, performance goal index data, information to do their own charting and indexing, and feedback on customer satisfaction. Second, the manager and the management team need to receive information from the self-directed team. The possibility of six to twenty self-directed teams operating and solving problems in a school creates both excitement and apprehension. The fact that the teams are improving the quality of the school is satisfying, but not knowing what they are doing creates uncertainty. Periodic reports, visits to the meetings, and copies of the minutes are minimum-communications channels that managers and management teams must have from self-directed teams. Third, the manager and the management teams should be prepared to support the self-directed teams, the success of which is their responsibility. Meeting-rooms, supplies, training, time for meetings, and celebrating success are only a few of the items that are the responsibility of management. If these are not addressed, the team may fall apart before it gets rolling. Fourth, the self-directed team needs to be delegated the authority to act without undue obstruction. This proviso often creates the difficult dilemma of how much authority to give a team, of course. Under boss management, self-directed teams almost always fail. There will be oversupervision of the team. Recommendations will be questioned. Fear will prevent information flow between the manager and the team. The loss of power by the team will cause a sense of frustration, the first hint of which will come when team members complain about the time spent in meetings. What they will really be complaining about is the waste of time in developing solutions that are not followed. When teams are not successful, the first place to look for the cause is lack of empowerment by management.

When is it time to stop mass inspection for quality? Mass inspection means (for example) testing all students, white-gloving all rooms, checking all buses, and grading all papers from a student. In the first place, one does not stop mass inspection until there is an organized (team-based) effort toward continuous improvement of the process. Only through a team effort can numerous ideas be generated in order to improve quality. The team must be empowered to act, must be supplied sufficient information, and must be trained, in order to have the essential elements for continuous improvement. During these stages the product or service must be mass-inspected to ensure quality. When the team begins functioning to the point where control charts, performance goal indicators, and other data show breakthrough toward quality standards, management then can move from mass inspection to random inspection of samples. The cost and waste of time spent in mass inspection can be reallocated to improving the process, thus reducing the cost even more. At some point, the team may expect to reach a standard of quality that makes further inspection redundant. That is the time to remove all end-of-line inspection, and rely on process and output data to be sure the process remains in control.

QUALITY CURVE

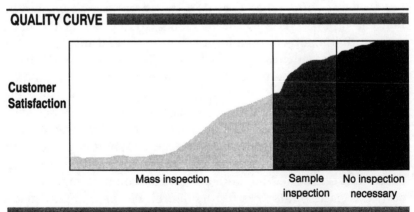

If effective communication takes place among the manager, the management team, and the self-directed teams, there is no need for the self-directed teams to report every decision. They should have the leeway to make changes to the process so long as policy or additional costs are not in question. Self-directed teams of teachers should have the authority to change the curriculum to make it more useful—to change instructional methodology, student schedules, special program assignment, modifications to any individual student curriculum, and student behavioral management, without seeking approval. How will management know, especially when some decisions may be controversial, affecting parents? If trust is present, the self-directed team will keep management informed through representatives, minutes, or reports. If the self-directed team has its own parent advisory committee, then most of these matters will be solved at the process level rather than at the management level. Self-directed teams are encouraged to meet periodically with customer advisory committees, to get feedback concerning proposals, recommendations, and the degree of customer satisfaction or dissatisfaction. The customers may be internal, external, or both. Oversupervising the team will result in distrust and the removal of risk-taking, in turn producing very little improvement of processes.

To implement self-directed teams, all four key ingredients must be present. Some may say this is not worth the hassle, but without self-directed teams, CIM as a philosophy essentially is untested. Only through process-based decision-making will true empowerment occur. To reach CIM, decisions must be made closest to the customer. These decisions are made by people who know their processes best. An organization needs to move to process-based decision-making using self-directed teams within six to four years, or face system decay from within.

Self-directed teams are voluntary. When the management team is ready to accept charters, any three to eight staff members with common processes or common customers may opt to form a team. There are three types of self-directed teams: process owner, cross-functional, and vertically integrated. *Process owner* teams are composed of members who have the same processes. *Cross-functional* teams are composed of members with the same customers, but possibly different processes. The members may be suppliers to other members. *Vertically integrated* teams are composed of managers and process owners. The team may be at a department or grade level, with the immediate supervisor involved on the team. There are advantages and disadvantages for each type of team. Vertically integrated teams can operate well with a lead manager. If not, then the team will only serve to do his/her bidding. Real empowerment can come from process owner or cross-functional teams. Of course, the effectiveness of the communication between management and the team is critical, since management is not part of the team structure.

Prospective team members should meet to develop an understanding of their system and to identify suppliers, supplier input, processes owned, products and services of these processes, and the customers. Current customer feedback mechanisms must be identified, and current partnerships with suppliers should be understood. System identification is important for many reasons. First, it tells the members what type of team they will have. It identifies the most critical focus of the team, the customer and the product or service. It helps the team to see whether there is adequate feedback in the system, and where partnerships can be improved. Last, it identifies the processes that will be improved.

The prospective team members will need to brainstorm their beliefs about customers, the customer services, and products of the team. These priority beliefs should be translated into a mission statement; the team's sole purpose is to fulfill this mission. The mission statement should be read at every meeting, and placed on all documents of importance. One short paragraph is appropriate for a mission statement.

With those preconditions met, the prospective team is ready to request a charter from the management team. Once that charter is received, the members should assign roles—either temporary on a rotated basis, or permanent as they see fit.

As a benchmark, the team should attach a performance goal index indicating measurement of success in terms of customer satisfaction and product quality. The performance index will indicate each year whether customer service and products have indeed improved, maintaining the focus on the customer. The performance goal index is always open for review by parents, managers, and the management team. The management team should periodically have the self-directed teams report on the progress they are making; the performance goal index is one way to show this progress.

A tough decision for the prospective team is whether or not to have a leader. Many self-directed teams have operated successfully without one. Members may choose to take turns facilitating the

REQUEST FOR SELF-DIRECTED TEAM CHARTER

Date of Request: _____

Name of Team: _____

List of process(es) that the team owns and plans to improve:

Mission of the team (regarding customer quality):

Team roles (can be rotated; members can have more than one role; however, each member should begin with at least one role):

ROLE   **TEAM MEMBER**

LEADER OR AGENDA PREPARER
*Responsible for agenda, time, place,
and keeping the meeting on task.*

FACILITATOR
*Responsible for using the TAPS Model
and Quality Process Control Tools.*

TIMEKEEPER/TASKMASTER
*Responsible for keeping the meeting
running on time and on task.*

RECORDER/SCRIBE
*Responsible for recording decisions and
other important information. Publishes minutes
for team members and MAT. Should
summarize the key points of the meeting
at the close of the meeting.*

TEAM WELFARE COORDINATOR
*Responsible for team spirit and needs of team,
such as refreshments, supplies, etc. Works with
leader to resolve conflicts. Develops plan for
celebrating success when achieved.*

CONSENSUS MAKER
*Responsible for being sure the team determines
how consensus will be decided before a
problem solving tool is used.*

DATA COLLECTOR
*Responsible for collection of data, or
coordinating data collection for the meeting.*

OTHER ROLES DECIDED BY TEAM:

Team meeting time, place, and day (recommended one hour per week on school time):

Signatures of Team Members:

1. _____
2. _____
3. _____
4. _____
5. _____
6. _____
7. _____
8. _____

Approval by Management Team: (check if 'yes'): ☐

Management Team Chairperson or Leader: _____

Date of Approval: _____

meeting and sharing other duties. Often these leaderless teams cooperate better in the long run than teams with leaders, because they learn to solve their own conflicts. However, leaders can give much-needed direction to the team, and keep it on task and using its tools. If the tools are not used, then time is usually wasted.

Once the management team has approved the self-directed team, the leader or agenda preparer should schedule the first meeting. The agenda should be similar to the following.

I. Reading of minutes of last meeting, and review/revision thereof

II. Individual assignment check

III. Identification and/or solving of problems

IV. Assignment of next meeting's needs

V. Summarization and assessment of meeting

VI. Confirmation of next meeting time, date, and place

The minutes of each meeting are necessary for continuity. Too, it gives the team a sense of accomplishment to review what occurred at the previous gathering. Minutes also are a valuable record of the team's decisions, and can be sent to both the management team and the parent advisory committee (if the team has one). To optimize time, data-gathering should be done outside of meeting time. Time should be allocated in the meeting for reports. Data should be in visual form, to allow members a clear view of them. The most important function is either problem identification or problem solving. The steps for problem identification should be followed in the first meeting; the team needs to get off on the right foot after organizing. Solving customer problems is its mission, and the tools for doing this must be used. Assignments are made for the next meeting if data need to be gathered. The summarizer should recap the meeting and hand out the assessment form. The time, date, and place of the next meeting should be announced. Then the meeting is over. A lot can be accomplished in an hour if the agenda and tools are efficiently utilized, so teams should endeavor to keep things moving right along between the starting and ending times.

TEAM ASSESSMENT

To determine conflicts, readiness, team problems, and the effectiveness of the meetings, an assessment needs to be given by each member at the end of the meeting. It should be anonymous, and summarized by the leader or agenda-preparer. The results should be placed in the minutes. If conflicts are apparent, time for conflict resolution should be allocated at the next meeting. The conflict should be expressed in words on a neutral communication format, such as an easel. The facilitator should request that the members write down on index cards what they believe are the causes. Each card should be read and discussed. If there are no solutions, the Six Hats tool can be used to brainstorm the issue and arrive at alternatives (green hat). If it continues to be a conflict, then the team should not be reluctant to call for outside help. The principal, or another staff member trained in conflict resolution, may be able to help the team to solve the problem.

Eventually, self-directed teams will handle their own budgets, keep their own control charts, and conduct their own customer interviews and surveys. If self-directed teams are not given their own budgets at formation, the management team should set aside an amount (such as $100) for supplies and a celebration. Several areas in the building should be reserved for team meetings. Easels, colored markers, paper, overhead projector, and a VCR need either to be in the room or available on request.

TEAM TRANSFORMATION

In a quality school, almost everyone eventually will be involved in volunteer self-directed teams. Morale will skyrocket as everyone begins teaming to continuously improve quality. The Four Quality Correlates will become a way of doing business. Students

ASSESSMENT OF TEAM AND MEETING

Meeting Effectiveness   Y or N

The meeting began on time.   ☐

The mission statement was read.   ☐

The minutes were read.   ☐

An agenda was prepared for everyone.   ☐

Problem solving tools were used.   ☐

The facilitator gave everyone a chance
  to participate.   ☐

The team used data rather than opinions.   ☐

The team examined causes
  rather than beginning with solutions.   ☐

Decisions made by consensus.   ☐

Everyone understands the process being studied.   ☐

Everyone was on task.   ☐

The meeting was summarized.   ☐

Outside team time assignments were made.   ☐

Conflicts, Problems or Concerns

It is time for a conflict resolution session?   ☐

The conflict is _____

It is time to have an open-agenda item for concerns.   ☐

This team has a problem we need to discuss.   ☐

Choose one: This team is forming,
  norming, storming, or performing.   [   ]

Incidentals

It is time for a celebration.   ☐

Everyone is performing his or her
  role satisfactorily.   ☐

Overall, the progress of this team is
  (S) satisfactory or (N) not satisfactory   ☐

will begin experiencing large measures of success, parents will be pleased, and employees happy. Self-directed teams will change the role of the manager and management team. Instead of fighting fires, the manager will work to support teams and keep the focus on the customer. The manager will supply teams with data on customer service and products. He or she will be visiting teams and helping to solve problems, but will never accept the responsibility for the problem. The manager will become (as it were) a coach getting the team ready for the big game. But this time all the players will be winners, and all will celebrate. Then the manager must, after each party, look again for opportunities to celebrate team success.

The management team eventually will find that there are fewer critical problems to solve, and will begin to concentrate on the trivial many—because even those can be chartered to existing self-directed teams. The need for chartering many teams for breakthrough will then become less and less, or at the very least the urgency will decrease.

PRINCIPAL PAT ANN HOLD

Pat was pleased with the training taking place on the campus. Almost all the staff were taking advantage of it. Staff members were teaching sessions in which they had some expertise. The management team had chartered numerous breakthrough teams to solve campus problems, and everyone was getting a chance to be on such a team. The quality initiatives were being implemented with action plans. Everything was going rather smoothly, except that Pat felt something was missing. She had moved from doing something to students and staff to doing for, and then with, them. She had become a good role model as a facilitator, listener, and questioner. She continued to remind the staff of the vision she had for the school: She believed they were on the way. Yet she was the instigator of most initiatives; she was still in the center ring. Everyone came to her with problems, seeking her advice and she wanted them to begin handling their own problems. She did not mind helping, but she certainly was ready to give them the responsibility. She then knew it was time to discuss with the management team the forming of self-directed teams. Pat wanted the teams to be called Team Approach to Problem Solving teams, or TAPS teams. This would focus attention on the teams' number one function. So, she developed a check sheet for the management team to review and discuss.

CHECK SHEET FOR FORMING TAPS TEAM

DONE

RESPONSIBILITIES OF MANAGEMENT TEAM AND PRINCIPAL

1. Useful customer and process data can be supplied to the TAPS team along with budget and costs information ☐

2. There is a procedure for obtaining useful information from the TAPS team ☐

3. Support for the TAPS team is ready in the form of: ☐

   a. Just-in-time training

   b. Supplies

   c. Meeting room

   d. Time for meetings

   e. Ways to celebrate success

4. Inspection for quality in determining the progress of the TAPS team is in place. ☐

5. The TAPS team will be given authority for the following: ☐

   a.

   b.

   c.

   d.

TAPS TEAM RESPONSIBILITIES

1. System Identification has been used to identify internal and external customers and suppliers and the input, processes owned, and output. ☐

2. A Mission Statement has been developed. ☐

3. A trained facilitator is a member of the team. ☐

4. Roles are assigned. ☐

5. Performance Goal Index is constructed. ☐

Pat knew a group of teachers who taught the same students and were sharing information at lunch. One of them was Will Survive, who was a real explorer when it came to quality in the classroom. She knew that TAPS teams should be voluntary, but she also knew it would only take a nudge for this group of teachers to volunteer to become the first TAPS team. And the first one needed to be successful. The proper hints were made, and the group not only accepted the challenge, but also completed their charter requirements in record time. They were then given authority to make any changes in the curriculum and instruction that would benefit students. They could also make schedule changes for students, as long as such affected only their classes. Too, they could set up their own student management system for behaviors that were not of the serious nature. Finally, they were given $100 for supplies, and assigned a meeting room.

The team agreed to meet on their lunch hour and after school. Pat promised them a common planning time in the next year if the team proved successful. The criteria indicators of success chosen by this TAPS team for the performance goal index were:

1. Average grade of all classes per teacher per grading period
2. Number of D's and F's per grading period
3. Average absences per grading period
4. Average tardies per grading period
5. Test scores on the state tests
6. Satisfaction level of students as measured by a survey given each grading period

Goals were set, and the ranges determined for progress. The criteria were weighted, and data were collected after each grading period. In addition, the teachers chose to keep control charts on their class grades, discipline problems, absences, and tardies.

The team was set to solve a problem. Pat cautioned the members to begin with a simple one that had a good chance at success. The team chose tardies, since that was not a big problem, but rather a nagging one. It collected data on the number of tardies, and interviewed a sample of students as to reasons therefore. Members made a flow diagram of the process for handling tardies, and discovered ways to streamline the process. The team brainstormed the causes, and reached consensus on the vital few. It also collected data on the vital few, using the flow diagram to determine where in the process to collect the data. The team analyzed these data, and generated possible solutions for correcting the causes. The vital few solutions were implemented using action plans. At last the control charts showed a breakthrough in the number of tardies. Pat took the team to dinner and a show, to celebrate the success. The team was anxious to try a tougher problem, one dealing with instruction and learning.

Pat had inquiries from other staff members asking to form a team. The management team decided it was time for such. Charters were made available to staff members, and a meeting was held with interested staff in order to go over the responsibilities. Eventually Pat gave Will and his team responsibility for their own budget. They could hire teachers if a vacancy occurred on their team. Maybe the day would come when the team could also fire a teacher who was not performing up to standards, Pat thought. The team determined its training needs, and members usually attended en masse. Members met three times a week, and once every two weeks there was a meeting for curriculum purposes, or a customer/supplier meeting with teachers in the previous grade or the following grade. It was not uncommon to find them meeting after hours, and sometimes on weekends. They were a team, and proud of it.

Pat was beginning to see signs of quality. Control charts were indicating breakthroughs in lowering defects and waste. Performance goal indexes were moving into the 800 and 900 ranges. New indexes were being created to continuously improve by beginning at the 300 level with the goals. Organizational health profiles were showing the organization to be very healthy. The number of TAPS teams was increasing, and they were beginning to improve the quality of their processes. The management team was functioning with very little guidance from Pat; they could operate often even without Pat being present. Best of all, the customer surveys indicated that customers were bragging about the school services and products. Students were achieving, and happy to be in a quality school. Failures and discipline problems were at an all-time low.

It had been a difficult journey, but Pat knew it had been worth it. She also knew that the task would never be over: Keeping CIM going would always be difficult, however much more enjoyable. But preventing fires was a lot more enjoyable than fighting them.

TEACHER WILL E. SURVIVE

Now that Will was member of a TAPS team, he was experiencing the happiest and most productive time of his life. The team had identified the vital few quality opportunities to study. The first priority was to increase student learning through improving the process of instruction. The project statement was to decrease the number of D's and F's in the team members' classes by improving the instruction. The team began with Six Hats to determine which data to collect. They interviewed students to find out what students thought about the current instruction, and they conducted educational diagnostic quality circles in order to gather data. The process flow diagram designed to help them to understand their process was difficult to work up. Each teacher had his or her own method of instruction, and that changed daily. They needed a process flow diagram for classifying what each did in the classroom. Madeline Hunter's lesson cycle fit the bill. It was not a way to teach, but rather a flow diagram of teaching acts that constitute everything a teacher can do in a classroom, or choose not to do. There were better ways to perform an act (according to the research), but not necessarily any wrong ways. The lesson cycle would allow each teacher to list the strategies used in each act.

The process flow diagram helped the team to brainstorm causes, using the cause-and-effect diagram. The effect was "problems with classroom instruction." The vital few for study were "Assessments not matching expected outcomes," "No reteach cycle," and "Ineffective independent practice." The team collected data on assessments made by the team members. Student assessments were sampled to examine the assessment items that were incorrect. The assessments were compared with the expected outcomes. The level of the assessments was analyzed using Bloom's taxonomy of cognitive skill levels, and the team discovered many discrepancies in the assessments in each class. The team first attended a workshop on assessing student learning, then devised a system for doing just that, using both authentic and simulated assessments, and aligning assessments with outcomes. All paper-and-pencil tests would henceforth be open-book tests; and there were other strategies developed by the team to correct the cause. It was a great start.

Will thought about how successful TAPS teams had been in the school. He wondered if students could also work in teams.

CLASSROOM LEARNING PROCESS

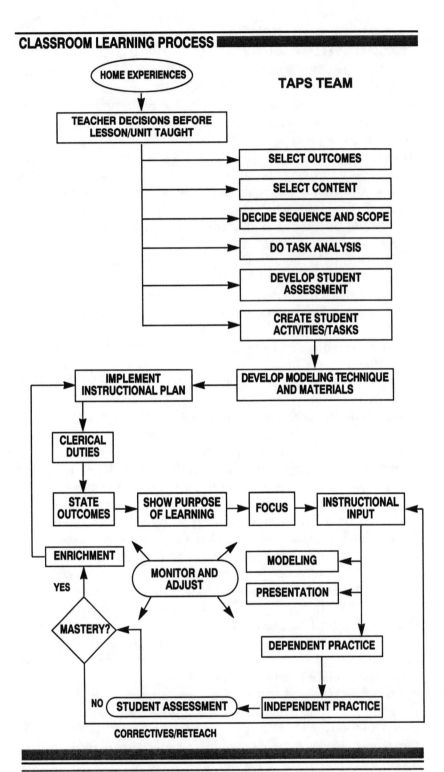

(They had worked very well in cooperative groups.) Learning teams would be a further step. He felt that his classes satisfied students' need for belonging, fun, and choices rather well. Learning teams would supply what athletic teams, band, and other extracurricular activities supply to the few who have the talent: Power in a fun manner. He might even create some friendly competition between the groups, as long as it wasn't related to their grades. Each month (or after agreed-on intervals of time) a contest between teams would be held. Parents would be invited. The teacher would be the questioner, and answers would be written down by all members of the team. A large plastic die would be rolled, to pick by chance which member of the team was to respond. There would be team problems, along with the individual responses. The scores would be totaled for an overall team score. Trophies would be awarded, and other recognition granted to winners. If a standard was to be set for points scored, then there could be more than one winner.

Learning teams would be responsible for the learning of all on the team. When a member was absent, it would be the team's responsibility to call that member, to give the assignments. On the next day, they would help the member with what had been covered. The team members would also help each other to understand the expected outcomes. Learning teams would solve problems, complete projects, assess their own quality, continuously improve their product, and even work cooperatively on assessments. If learning could be made useful and enjoyable, then the chances for real life learning would be greatly enhanced. Will could not wait for the next school year to begin.

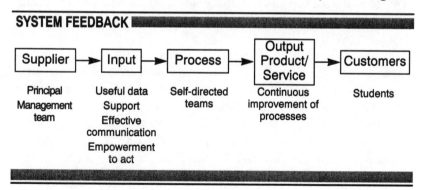

SYSTEM FEEDBACK

Supplier	→	Input	→	Process	→	Output Product/ Service	→	Customers

| Principal Management team | Useful data Support Effective communication Empowerment to act | Self-directed teams | Continuous improvement of processes | Students |

THE DICKINSON EXPERIENCE

The Dickinson Independent School District piloted TAPS teams with a group of bus mechanics who chose to become a team rather than have a supervisor. This team completed its charter and presented it to the transportation department for approval. The management team supplied this team with a computer and a budget for supplies. (The computer was used to keep control charts and data on buses and customer service.) A survey was given to a sample of bus drivers every two weeks, to discover the quality of service by the mechanics. The team met every week for a couple of hours, to review data and use the TAPS model to solve the vital few problems. The role of leader was rotated each six months. Two trained facilitators were members of the team. Training was provided to members who attended a workshop on teaming skills. The team's data indicated that two buses were needing a disproportionate amount of repairs. After brainstorming causes, corrections were made. Customer service improved, and everyone appeared to be satisfied with the results.

Another TAPS team was begun with building keepers at the high school. Without using a facilitator, the team met for four months to develop a plan for cleaning the building. The final plan was a consensus of all members, or at least it so appeared. However, problems arose immediately after the plan was adopted. Two members made excuses not to follow the plan. No time was set aside for meetings to communicate the problems. The line of communication was blurred for obtaining supplies, equipment repairs, and building maintenance items. The leader worked only the day shift, so he did not communicate with the night crew. And teaming to clean the building was not discussed.

Since there was no system for inspecting the building for cleanliness, the team foundered, then sank into oblivion. While the motives of all involved were worthy, the implementation was flawed. First, either consensus was not reached, or else two members regularly disrupted the process. When a problem arose, there were no means by which to address the causes, complicated by the fact that the team did not have a regular time to meet. There was no chance to cooperate, because everyone had pressing duties.

The team was not ready for self-assessment of its own quality; mass inspection of the building was needed. (This could have been done by the lead building keeper and operations supervisor.) There were no checks to see if quality was occurring, nor was there a feedback system for communicating to the building keepers problems concerning cleanliness. In short, the four points of teaming were not followed. There was no support, no communication, too much empowerment without inspection, and a lack of data by process owners.

The support department staffs of food service, transportation, and maintenance and operations were very receptive to CIM. They valued training, and were conscious of what quality could mean in their positions and in the departments. They took their tasks with breakthrough teams and management teams seriously. The support departments were similar to the industrial systems around Dickinson that were using CIM; the staff members could readily transfer the CIM model for industry to their department and needs. As a result, the support departments were excellent sites wherein to try CIM principles and operate TAPS teams. What was learned there served the district well when implementing CIM at the campuses.

The secretarial staff was yet another source for TAPS teams and continuous improvement for quality. A group of secretaries in the educational support center formed a team, the intent being to improve the process for preparing board agenda manuals for the twice-a-month board meetings. The team used the TAPS model one hour per week for four months. There were times when they chose to meet more than once a week. The team gave the board their product as a booklet containing their customer data, a process flow diagram, a cause–effect diagram, a Pareto diagram of the vital few causes, and recommendations. An example of the new format for the board manual was presented to board members, who approved the recommendations for a trial period of three months. During that time, the team would collect data from the users and suppliers, make revisions if necessary, and then report to the board. The data showed an overwhelming support for the new procedures and format.

MANAGEMENT PRINCIPLES

ORGANIZING

Training for team members; meeting place and time; a facilitator; communication between manager, management team, and self-directed team; useful information from manager and management team to self-directed team; support; and when to celebrate suc-cess—all are key functions and elements of organizing.

PLANNING

Use SPC tools to follow the plan-do-check/study-act out-line.

CONTROLLING

Performance goal index developed by self-directed team as a self-assessment of their quality; control charts by management and the team members; and inspection methods by the manager, until quality standards are met—all are methods of controlling.

LEADING

Empowerment of the team to make decisions affecting members' processes; conflict resolution by the manager; using tools; and reality therapy and quality circle problem-solving technique—all are lead management principles to use with self-directed teams. The manager must be prepared to give the team complete authority to change members' processes, as long as the team uses the tools and the changes do not produce costs beyond its budget, or affect other teams or departments. The manager can expect the team to survey its customers, before implementation, to discover if there are any obstacles.

CHAPTER 11

System in Action for Continuous Improvement

Once placed in action, a CIM system will cause gradual, at times almost imperceptible, change. With the exception of revolution and coups d'état, few fundamental shifts occur overnight. Certainly the business of replacing a century-old model of schooling with a streamlined 1990s version is not one that occurs in a year, or even five years. Progress is not a straight upward curve; it's more like a stream that doubles back and forth on its way toward the sea of quality. School districts moving toward CIM will travel through much the same stages, as described in this chapter (see Hershey and Blanchard's situational leadership theory). Coercive, noncoercive, and permissive leadership can be explained through use of the leadership styles and readiness levels of the worker.

HERSHEY AND BLANCHARD'S SITUATIONAL LEADERSHIP THEORY

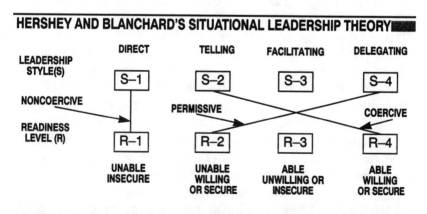

The first stage of readiness or maturity is "unable and insecure." The insecure workers can be either stubborn individuals or groups that fear risk-taking and change and are resistant because of (e.g.) personal problems or stress. "Unable" can be the result of a lack of training, the need for new skills, or the absence of understanding of the job requirements. The arbitrator's appropriate leadership style for the "unable and insecure" is a direct one. It is a *high-task, low-relations* style that involves doing most of the preparation and planning while receiving little feedback from the workers. The manager usually tells the workers, by using clear and precise directions, what to do. Most inexperienced workers fall in this readiness stage, although experienced workers can drop back to this stage when change occurs. This stage also applies to those workers who refuse to use their skills for various reasons.

The second stage of readiness is "unable but willing." The motivation for these workers is belonging and caring. To use Glasser's control theory terms, the worker is "controlling for belonging." The appropriate leadership style is *high-task, high-relations*. The leader serves as a negotiator, constantly selling or convincing. When workers recognize that there is trust present, they will be willing—although usually not completely able—to do the work or accept the change. The worker is waiting to be sold on the new skills needed. The leader must be well-prepared and organized (and receive ample feedback from the worker) in order to negotiate the training needed for the change. The key is trust. It takes a lead manager to develop the right climate. However, some workers who have lived under a system of distrust for long periods will choose not to trust others. They will remain in Stage One until peer pressure moves them to Stage Two or they quit, retire, or are fired.

Stage Three is the "able but unwilling or insecure" phase. These workers are controlling for esteem and power. The lead manager will respond to these workers as a mediator or facilitator, which requires a *low-task, high-relations* style. This stage usually occurs when workers have been sold on changes or training, but are then either reluctant or unsure of how to use their newly acquired skills. This stage can occur when experienced workers go through a period of low motivation or "being in a rut." They are ready for new challenges, but must become involved with others in order to see the purpose before plunging in. The leader should get ample feedback, then use group processes and a participatory style to bring the worker back on track. The manager must satisfy, with recognition for the worker's successes, the worker's need for power.

The fourth stage is the ideal stage, "able and willing." The worker is controlling for fun and choices, and so the required leadership style is *low-task, low-relations.* The worker is ready for independent work, and satisfies his or her basic needs through these efforts. The leader who delegates responsibility and authority to the Stage Four worker will produce a worker who assesses his or her own quality of work and continuously improves it. This worker will receive fun and freedom through performing in teams and using quality improvement skills. The Stage Four worker not only embraces change, but encourages more of it.

Lead managers attempt to meet the needs for which workers are controlling, so that they can progress toward the "able and willing" readiness level. The effective lead manager recognizes the readiness level of the worker and his or her need to satisfy. That manager can best accomplish this by matching the proper leadership style with the readiness level. This is noncoercive leadership. The lead manager is continually getting feedback from workers, to test whether the leadership style is matching the maturity/readiness level. If it is not, that manager shifts to the proper style of leadership.

Managers can overestimate or underestimate the readiness style of the workers. If the manager underestimates, he or she runs the risk of being perceived as coercive. For example, if an individual or group is willing and able, but the leader uses a participatory style instead of delegating, some members will think they are being coerced by being held back from working independently. There will be a feeling of mistrust by the workers in reaction to a perceived lack of trust by the manager in not allowing them the freedom and fun of working either as a team or as individuals independently. This is true for any stage of readiness if the manager underestimates the level by applying a lower level of leadership style. If the manager misjudges the level of readiness by two stages, then most workers will perceive the leader as coercive. For example, if the workers are ready for the participatory style and the leader is in a telling mode, the result is almost always distrust by the workers because they believe they are being coerced.

When the manager overestimates the readiness level, the leader runs the risk of being perceived as permissive. The leader who uses a participatory, negotiative, or delegative style on "unable and insecure" workers will be labeled as permissive by some persons, depending on how far removed the style is from the readiness level. Workers will take advantage of the permissive manager. Permissiveness is not noncoercive management. Permissiveness is either overestimating the maturity or readiness level, or not wanting to face an issue by moving down to the proper level of leadership style. Permissive leadership can be more destructive in some cases than can coercive boss management.

While boss managers continually underestimate the readiness level of their workers, they tend to spend most of their time in the telling or selling mode. Under boss managers, the workers rarely as individuals (and never collectively) move upward in the maturity or readiness stages. In fact, they become entrenched in the "unable and insecure" stage. They become comfortable with the direct style of the manager, and are ready to let him or her do everything. We often hear the boss manager accurately say, "I have to do everything in this organization." Quality change virtually never happens under a boss manager, because that manager mandates change rather than fosters it. When a lead manager is faced with "unable and insecure" workers, he or she must shift to a very direct manner of leadership. This is *not* coercion, although workers knowledgeable of lead management theory may use the excuse that it *is*. The other workers will not perceive the style as coercion, but rather as effective leadership. When the workers move past the first stage, they will look back and agree it was the best style for the situation. The key is for the lead manager to move to selling and negotiating when the reluctant and untrained worker is ready to move to Stage Two. Leaders who spend too much time directing in the first stage run the risk of being perceived as coercive when the individual, team, or staff is controlling for belonging. Good managers know their subordinates and understand their readiness level.

Teachers, as managers, can use Hershey and Blanchard's theory to understand how their students move through different stages. It is the duty of the lead teacher to move students to the "able and willing" stage, where they are assumed to be self-directed learners. Boss teachers operate almost exclusively in the telling mode by lecturing, using work sheets, controlling by rules, and always acting as if they must do something to the student. "Able and willing" students feel oppressed by this style.

The "unable and insecure" students feel comfortable and, as a result, don't acquire the needs of belonging, esteem, fun, and choices that students need to achieve in the real world. The comfortable student in Stage One finds excuses to do below-standard work because it fits his or her role as an unsuccessful student. Boss teachers want more rules, more punishments, and more done to the students to get them to work or to behave properly. Theirs is a cycle that never ends, and does not produce quality for the majority of students.

The permissive teacher tries to involve students and relax expectations with a Stage One class—often with disastrous results. He or she follows the disaster with complaints that the new way of managing does not work. Teachers, like administrators, must learn to match the readiness/maturity level with their management style. With "unable and insecure" students, the teacher must choose a more direct style of management. He or she must provide structure, be organized, and give clear, precise directions to the students. The teacher must then begin to work on satisfying the students' needs for belonging. When they are ready for this, the teacher must move to either a negotiating or a selling mode. It is now time to get feedback from the students, through quality circle meetings and class discussions. The lead teacher recognizes when the need for belonging is nearly satisfied, and moves to Stage Three with its more participatory style—using cooperative learning and supplying the need for power through cooperative efforts.

Students must be recognized for their achievements in other ways than grades. Before long, they will be ready for independent work with its few rules and restrictions. These are the students who can assess their own work for quality, and continuously improve it. What is needed is more lead teachers, those who can move students to this last level in a school year. The assessment of a teacher's worth is his or her ability to move to an enabling or delegating style without using coercion or permissiveness.

ASSESSING READINESS LEVELS
WORK ON THE SYSTEM: READINESS LEVEL 1
In implementing CIM, the manager of the organization or classroom should assess the readiness level of the workers, staff, or students. Most workers will be in the first stage of understanding and using CIM, probably greeting it with a mixture of skepticism and unconcern, believing it to be just another program that

will soon be shelved to make way for another change. Since they do not have the advanced skills, the manager must begin at their level. It is time to utilize Correlate One, *Work on the System*. The manager must focus on a set vision for the journey, but usually will get little feedback as yet. He or she must expend large amounts of time telling everyone what the vision means, and how it can be accomplished. The workers need to know that the manager has a plan, and can begin to trust that he or she knows where this will lead. They now are controlling for security. Will the change mean they will lose their job? What impact will CIM have on them? These and other security questions need to be answered by the manager. The workers must be assured that CIM is not just another program, but a fundamental mind-set change regarding how public schooling operates.

All employees should begin studying the Four Correlates. General training should begin immediately, with either a steering committee or the whole staff. The manager must be center-stage in the training, always available to help others learn the concepts. The same principle applies in the classroom, too. The teacher should begin training the students for the move to a quality classroom; classroom training should focus on understanding the system the workers work in. The discussion of quality should continue over a period of time, up to a full school year.

Most educators will be thinking for the first time about concepts such as "Who are my customers and suppliers?" and "What inputs, processes, and outputs are parts of the system?" The very idea that quality is determined by the customer and not the producer is foreign to many people. It sounds permissive to those who believe they have the answers. One must continue to ask "How did you get the answers without asking the customers?" It's a question that even the diehard stimulus–response proponents cannot answer.

When workers begin to understand how their systems work, the manager should lead them in developing a mission statement. The mission should tell what the new system will do for the customers. The mission statement, which describes the outputs that will satisfy all customers, should begin with an examination of the beliefs of the staff regarding quality service, quality products, and customer satisfaction.

This is true in the classroom, too. The teacher needs to begin training the students for the quality classroom. Most students at the beginning of a new term are reluctant learners who do not know what is in store for them. Their trust level is usually low. Many teachers make the mistake of beginning with assignments and the curriculum. Teachers who want quality must first establish the purpose of the subject, the usefulness of the learning, and the procedures for the classroom. Until meaning is established, students will not see a need to do quality work. Some successful teachers have taken as long as three weeks to establish the relevancy of the learning. This initial period helps the teacher to know the strengths of the students, and helps them to get acquainted with the teacher.

It is a time to set the ground rules for the class. The teacher should post a few standards of behavior expected in class, and then ask for standards of behavior for the teacher. Both should be posted for all to see. The teacher should set the stage for working out conflicts by stating that if there is a problem with any of the standards, either the teacher or the student can ask for a conference. This should take place in the conference area of the classroom reserved for this purpose. In this manner, the teacher has established how problems will be solved in this class.

All rules and procedures for homework, grades, learning assessments, and tardies/absences should be explained. The students are looking for structure and security in this new environment. Teachers should require students to help with the routines of the classroom, such as checking roll, taking up absent slips, etc. and begin class each day with distributive practice over old learning. This review reinforces old learning and gives the teacher a chance to prepare for the day while students are working. It cuts down on tardies in secondary schools if points are given for correct responses.

Early in the year, the teachers should lead the students in defining quality and why quality is important. They should identify who their customers are and who the suppliers are. They should discuss the processes owned by the students, and which inputs and outputs are important. When the students' reluctance begins to disappear, the teacher should begin using quality circle discussions once every week or two. The teacher should begin by using open-ended circles. At the end of each unit, a diagnostic quality circle should be conducted to assess the unit's effectiveness. When problems arise involving the whole class, a problem-solving quality circle using the steps of reality therapy may help.

The teacher should explain to students how to goal-set, using the plan-do-check/study-act cycle and require them to develop their goals for the year or term. He or she should lead them in brainstorming their beliefs about learning and classroom outputs. From their beliefs, the teacher should develop a mission statement for the classroom, and post it. The teacher must find times to talk with students one-on-one about their beliefs and the mission, beginning with the opinion leaders first (the students after whom everyone else models his or her behavior). The teacher is building trust, especially with those who may model negative behavior. The teacher must recognize effort rather than ability: Quality will come with effort, not because of ability.

ADOPT LEAD MANAGEMENT PRINCIPLES: READINESS LEVEL 2

When the staff begins to understand and feel comfortable with CIM, the manager should shift from a directing and telling style to a selling style. Selling requires the manager's direct involvement in training, planning, and receiving feedback from the workers. The manager must develop ways to get input from workers and customers alike. This is a time when the staff is controlling for belonging or involvement, so the manager should respond by including the staff in the planning for quality. All staff members must be trained in control theory, and should realize that humans choose behaviors to satisfy the needs of fun, belonging, power, freedom, and survival. We form quality pictures in our head that best satisfy our needs. When we choose behaviors that produce relationships, activities, or situations that compare favorably with our quality pictures, then we are in control of our lives. When our chosen behaviors produce relationships, activities, or situations that do not satisfy our pictures of what we really want in our lives, we begin controlling for the need that is not satisfied. If we choose behaviors that continue to cause conflict in our life, we have the feeling of being out-of-control. Only when we satisfy this need will we regain control of our lives. Unless others help us to choose better alternatives, we often choose very destructive behaviors as we run out of choices.

All workers have pictures in their minds of a need-fulfilling workplace. When the workplace is ruled by a boss manager, the needs of the workers become subservient to the manager's needs. Boss managers attempt to motivate by fear. They offer rewards and punishments in an effort to control people. Fear inhibits the workers' ability to choose productive behaviors; they choose to do only enough to satisfy the manager. The manager becomes the customer, and the real customer suffers. Workers will not do quality work when work under a boss manger does not match up with one of their quality pictures. Any implementation of the Four Quality Correlates will be a failure. Workers also will not assess their own quality, because of the fear that the data will be used to evaluate performance. Nor will they perform effectively in teams, because they do not feel they will be delegated the authority to make process improvement decisions, or contributions that will be recognized. Because boss managers foster competition among workers, and thrive on win/lose situations, the cooperation and trust needed for continuous improvement problem-solving will not be present. The losers will choose sabotaging behaviors, and behaviors that cause low morale and conflicts, in their attempt to gain power and belonging.

Lead managers create workplaces where trust is present and where the needs of the workers are satisfied. Only in this climate will workers choose quality-producing behaviors. Work will not be need-fulfilling unless it is enjoyable and provides recognition for the worker's efforts. Lead mangers know this, and make work meaningful for the workers. They give them choices, and develop a cooperative environment that enhances teaming. Workers under lead managers put the workplace, and eventually their work, in their quality picture album. Even more important, they put the manager in their quality world. These workers will be willing to expend the efforts to improve quality for the school, the manager, and the feeling of doing a job well.

As a school moves to CIM using noncoercive management principles, the workers will begin to respond to the change. They will resist any attempt to change back. Boss managers can survive in a school where boss management is the prevailing way to manage. However, when most managers in the system practice lead management principles, boss managers become dinosaurs. The workers can see how they themselves fare under lead management, and will rebel against boss management. Unless boss managers change in a noncoercive system, they will go the way of the dinosaur, except for fighting all the way. This phenomenon will occur in any system if enough managers will adopt the lead management principles.

To help sell the Four Quality Correlates, the manager must use data. Data showing the poor quality of current products and services will help people to see the need to change. In school systems with large dropout rates, expulsions and absenteeism should suffice to indicate that the system is "broke." There will of course be resistance to the facts by those who will compare their school to others, proving in their minds that everyone is in the same boat. Involvement is the key to overcoming this obstacle: Bring the resisters into the plans for CIM and implementation of the quality correlates. Training in lead management and control theory must be continuous, and everyone in the system should be involved in it. All managers should complete 24 clock-hours of training in lead management and control theory in the initial stages, followed by refresher and advanced courses each year.

In the classroom, the teacher needs to practice lead management principles if students are expected to do quality work. When students enter kindergarten, they are eager to learn. They find a need-satisfying classroom, which is why practically all students love kindergarten. They put a halo around the picture of the teacher in their minds. Recess, new friends, creative work at classroom centers, and even nap time help form a positive school picture. There is a sense of belonging, choices, and fun. And the student receives ample recognition for his/her work. Above all, he or she knows that school is the only place that teaches students what adults already know: Reading. Reading means power— the power to read books, newspapers, and comics.

By the third grade, though, some of the halos are tarnished. Reading is not as enjoyable, because the student is in a lower group or doesn't receive the gold stars like other students. The student then finds little power in reading, and begins to look for other ways besides learning to satisfy this need. By the fifth or sixth grade, most of the pictures of learning, reading, and the teacher as a need-satisfying person have been totally removed. The student is satisfying his or her needs in ways not connected with the classroom. School may still have a halo if the need for friends is being met, but by the eighth grade, even school has been removed from many students' quality pictures. These students are planning to drop out either physically or, if forced to stay, mentally. School as a need-satisfying place has now been replaced by gangs and parties, and perhaps also drugs and alcohol, as ways to satisfy the need for power and belonging. Other students have learned to do "good enough" work to keep teachers and parents satisfied and off their backs. Very few are doing quality work, because it is not required and the learning is not very useful or enjoyable.

When the students are in the "unable but willing" stage, the teacher should begin introducing them to the Quality Classroom Correlates. They should be taught control theory, the principles of lead management, and reality therapy counseling. Survey the students on their needs, expectations, how they like to be taught, and what is important to them. Involve them in the learning process by appointing, on a rotating basis, peer tutors and teacher assistants. The peer tutors will help individuals when they are having learning difficulties. Teacher assistants will help the teacher with the teaching duties. They can present lessons, develop visual aids, and work with groups. Stage One is also the time to negotiate new rules and procedures set by the teacher. He or she should occasionally have students self-assess their work for quality, and should continually ask "Why?" when rating their work as quality. Begin using cooperative learning groups, starting with pairs and eventually working up to groups of four.

Homework is one of the most destructive things that schools can perpetrate when students are required to fill in repetitive work sheets that require little thinking. Students turn off from homework because it seems like busy work. When many students fail to do the work, ask them about their perception of the work. Most will say it adds little value to their learning. Begin assigning homework that requires thinking skills for extra credit. Ask students to do an activity with their parents, or make an assignment where they have to show their parents how to do something the student has learned in school. Ask the students to watch a special TV program, and follow up with a quality circle meeting, to discuss the program. With a lead teacher who introduces these quality classroom correlates, the students will feel a sense of belonging—an ownership in the class—and will begin viewing work as need-satisfying.

ASSESS OWN QUALITY: READINESS LEVEL 3
In the change to quality there will come a time when the worker is able through training to accomplish the transformation, but is unwilling for fear of failure. The worker is controlling for power — success and recognition. The manager must create success by placing the worker on teams, and providing the tools and support that guarantee success. It is time to test the trust level by allowing the workers or teams of workers to assess their own quality. Allowing workers or teams to assess their own quality is true empowerment. They will need training in utilizing statistical process control tools and performance goal indexes. The manager needs to eliminate the fear in the system that comes from evaluations, rankings, and merit pay systems based on the perceived performance of the worker.

The manager should continue his/her own measurements of the process and of the quality of the product or service. However, he or she needs to recognize the difference between special causes and common causes. Special causes need to be solved in conferences with the workers who know the problem best. Common causes should be addressed by organizing teams to solve the problem. This involvement in team problem-solving will help workers to become more willing to make the change to CIM. Placing the workers on management teams or break-through teams, and conducting quality circle meetings to discuss issues, will replace their fear of failing with a feeling of partici-pation and cooperation with others. System planning is an excel-lent method for involving all the workers in setting the course for the quality initiatives that will create a quality school.

When teachers introduce new ways of teaching, or managing the classroom, students may experience an unwillingness to try them out. There is a fear of taking risks, of moving away from the old ways, and of what the impact of that will be on them. The teacher must get the students involved in the changes. Training in the new skills is essential, but students must also see the need for the use of these skills in their lives and future work. Cooperative learning should be an integral part of the classroom, promoting positive interdependence and individual accountability. Students should develop criteria for quality in major assignments, and should be allowed to rate models of work, using the criteria. They then should rate their own work for quality, using the agreed-on criteria.

The teacher should look for ways to reduce the reliance on grades by teaching students to use control charts in order to record their own grades, contracting for grades (with only A or B work accepted), or replacing grades with demonstrations of mastery of learning. To demonstrate mastery, the students must to be able to show how they accomplished the task, and answer questions per-taining to what was learned. Certificates of mastery could take the place of grades, or the student and teacher might agree on whether the learning is at either a competent or a quality level. Anything else would need improvement.

Students need to see that only quality work is good enough, because only it produces pride of workmanship. At first, students may not do quality work in the eyes of the teacher, but with fair critiques that are noncoercive, students will begin taking bigger risks, and be more creative in their work. After years of "Good enough will do," it is difficult to think in terms of quality. It is the duty of the teacher to influence the students to place quality work in their quality world.

The teacher needs to become a facilitator of learning rather than a possessor of all the knowledge. Only through facilitating will students go beyond comprehension and recall, and on to higher-order thinking skills. Each student must seek his or her own limits, but with encouragement will even stretch those limits. As long as the teacher is the center of the classroom, this will not happen. The classroom must be child-centered. It is time for students to have more choices: Learning should be a lot more fun to the students in the class.

CONTINUOUS IMPROVEMENT OF QUALITY: READINESS LEVEL 4

The workers are now at the enabling stage. It is time for their continuous improvement of processes to produce quality products and service. Training in quality process control tools and the team approach to problem-solving methods is a must for the workers: They are ready for self-directed teams. Lead management has produced a trust level which teams can operate efficiently. Team members are given the authority to make decisions without requesting approval. The workers are controlling for fun and choices. Self-directed teams will satisfy both needs if organized appropriately by management.

The workers need relevant data and other information from management to self-assess the quality of the process and improve it. They are prepared for an all-out effort to improve the quality of the school. The manager should delegate both the power to change the processes, and the responsibility to improve them. He or she needs to communicate often with the teams, to help them over hurdles and give them needed support. The manager must also now be alert to teams' reverting to previous stages of readiness. Training in team-building skills will help prevent teams from becoming unwilling (or even unable) to use the tools. Every team's responsibility is to use the tools to plan-do-check/study-act for continuous improvement. The manager should keep the focus of the teams on the customer and the mission.

Students who are "able and willing" should be the goal of every teacher. A school of able and willing students is a quality school. Students should be asked to self-assess the quality of their work, and then improve it. Homework should be for improving their work. Students should be organized into learning teams responsible for the learning of everyone on the team.

There should be friendly competition between the teams, in the pursuit of quality. Students and teams alike should be given the freedom to make their own choices of how to accomplish the work. The content should be taught through problem-solving units. Problems can be simulated, but real-life problems should be the goal. Students should be allowed to continuously improve their grades or work—even test results.

The teacher is a coach, giving help only when needed. He or she relies on questioning skills to find out how the student teams are doing. This teacher has prepared his/her students for the real world of work in the twentieth century. These are the students who can work cooperatively in teams to improve quality in our companies and government. They will have the training and initiative to take on the challenging tasks facing our nation. They will have the self-esteem to overcome boss management and stimulus–response approaches to solving problems. Better yet, they will be the managers of the future.

Workers going through change, such as the movement to a quality school through using CIM, may not be able to move smoothly from one stage of readiness to the next. There are many variables involved, and each school is different. The workers may for example jump or fall back one or two stages at any time. A lead manager will see any of this coming, and be prepared to use the proper leadership style to get the workers moving toward more effective behaviors. Change is like grief: There is anger, denial, acceptance, and support, before initiating change. The change to CIM management will cause many workers to go through all these stages. Lead managers can however help make each stage a short one.

REFINEMENT OF CONTINUOUS IMPROVEMENT

With the implementation of all quality initiatives, including self-directed teams, the system should begin showing improvement in quality. The outcomes expected of students should begin meeting business, college, and other external customer requirements. This is no time for resting; however, the time involved in firefighting should be diminishing, and planning time increasing. Managers will find that most of their time is spent in teams developing preventive measures. The manager must keep reminding him/herself that this is better than the old method of putting out fires by crisis management. The difficult time for managers is when both are occurring—the fires and time spent in prevention. This time will come after three or four years of implementing the quality initiatives. In fact, fires that were hitherto hidden from the manager because of fear will now combust. This is a critical time for the manager, whether it is while managing the school or the classroom. The manager will feel that there is not enough time to do everything. Does he/she correct problems, or prevent them? The manager cannot simply ignore the problems that surface: The problem-solving tools should be used, even though they require more time than is used in merely throwing solutions at a problem. The solutions using the tools will be consensus decisions and will be supported, as opposed to the tendency to apply "band-aids" that require more time in the long run. The manager must keep the faith and strive to fulfill the vision of a quality school or classroom. The journey is well worth the time and effort. In a quality school or classroom, time will be spent mostly in enjoyable experiences. You must cross the mountains of change before coming to the valley of quality.

ORGANIZATIONAL CHART FOR PROCESS-BASED DECISION-MAKING

The organizational chart of a quality school should be similar to the one following.

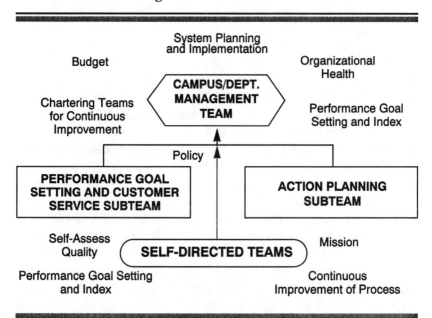

There should be less need for supervisors and mid-level managers in a quality school than in other types. Teams will take over the functions that were in the past delegated to these managers. The organization should become flatter, with a lower level of bureaucracy. This change will improve the communication and the speed with which decisions can be made. The savings can be used to increase the staff development budget.

DISTRIBUTION OF POWER FOR CONTINUOUS IMPROVEMENT

How much power should managers give management teams and self-directed teams? This is a tough question to answer. There are usually two parts to every quality improvement problem. One part is the "what" and the other is how will the "what" be delivered. Decisions need to be made regarding what needs to take place, or what the product or service should look like, and then decisions made on how it will be delivered. The "what" requires attention to customer needs. The quality initiatives are the "whats" that need to take place before quality can be addressed. Other "whats" are structure changes, such as interdisciplinary teaming, heterogeneous grouping, ungraded classes, and multiage classes. Many of these decisions are made by managers and management teams because they are involved in collecting the data from the customers. However, self-directed teams that survey and get feedback from their customers may make "what" type decisions. How the "what" is delivered is a decision best made by process owners. Sometimes the managers are the process owners, but more than likely the workers own the process. The following diagram illustrates the relationship between "what needs to be done" decisions and "how it should be done" decisions. Who usually makes these decisions is shown, with managers making more "what" decisions than "how," and self-directed teams just the opposite. As self-directed teams become more proficient, they too may take on more "what" decisions, of course.

Before "what" type decisions are made, ample input from the process owners must be obtained. The best decision is one reached with consensus between management and the process owners. However, there are times when management must decide what needs to happen for the improvement of quality to the customer. If the decision is based on anything but customer quality improvement, then it is self-serving and will destroy trust. Discussion and ground rules must be laid as to who will make which decisions, or else conflicts will occur between managers and teams.

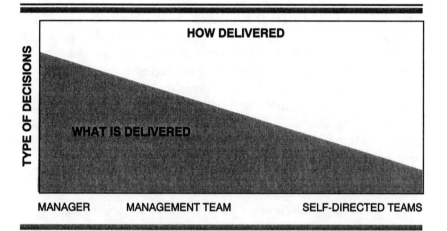

MANAGEMENT TEAM FOCUS ON DISCIPLINE PROBLEMS

When management teams are formed, their first inclination is to solve problems that benefit the members more than the customers. If these problems will help to improve the organizational health, then they may prove worthwhile. It is natural for management teams to select discipline as a vital few problem to solve. The sore point is that it is not a customer-focused problem, it rarely addresses the real causes, and (subsequently) rarely do the offered solutions work. Many times, in fact, the solutions are additional rules or punishments, rather than improved discipline. By definition, discipline is the ability to choose proper behavior for the time and situation. Discipline implies a learning of which behaviors to choose. It must be taught. Punishment, on the other hand, is something we do to students with the student having no (or very few) choices in the matter. There is no teaching involved in punishment.

Most systems selected by site-based decision-making teams ignore the teaching and learning of behavior that produces discipline. The solution often is what we will do to students, a stimulus–response approach with rewards and punishments for good and bad behavior respectively. If students are not taught, or if counseling is left out of the solution, then punishment will be perceived as coercive by the students, and "good enough" behavior is all that can be expected of them. The "good enough" behavior will occur only through close supervision and mass inspection, all this creating a huge waste of manpower and time. When the students are not supervised, they will revert to behaviors that cause vandalism, fighting, and other unproductive results. It reminds one of the teacher who operates as a boss manager in the telling stage all during the year. He or she may be able to control the students by constant surveillance in the classroom, but pity the substitute who comes in when the boss teacher is missing.

The solution is to select problems that have more payoff for the customer. If a school can implement strategies that move students toward the "able and willing" stage, that encourage doing things with the students, that satisfy the needs of the students, and that help to create a curriculum, and to develop trained lead teachers who provide useful learning, then eventually a system of discipline can be selected that matches these objectives.

An effective discipline system involves the following:

1. Counseling involving both reality therapy and constructive feedback
2. Choices for the student and teacher alike
3. Conferencing between the only ones who can work out the problem: the teacher and the student
4. Training for the teacher
5. The setting—by the students—of the standards, the few rules needed, and even the consequences
6. The elimination of punishment and coercion by using time, choices, and teaching styles to make better plans
7. Support by a critical mass of the students, teachers, and administrators

Staff must realize that, until most teachers are using lead management principles by moving students to an "able and willing" stage, then no system will work. If there were a system that worked with "unable and insecure" students, then everyone would be using it. Instead, the solution is to get rid of these students. The problem is that until the system changes, there will always be more irresponsible students to take the place of those who were removed. What a waste! Unfortunately, there are no easy solutions: Punishment is easy, but only reinforces the belief of those who are continually irresponsible that they are failures. Teaching discipline requires time and energy—but the results are more than worth the effort.

AUDITING FOR ASSESSMENT OF CONTINUOUS IMPROVEMENT INITIATIVES

Schools should invite experts in CIM to audit them periodically. Too often those inside the school cannot see the forest for the trees; everything may appear to be going well. However, an audit by outside experts will give the school a thorough report of what it is doing well, and what needs study. The audit should focus on the Four Quality Correlates and how well they are being utilized. The following is a list of questions that auditors can use to assess the organization.

CAMPUS/DEPARTMENT QUALITY AUDIT

I. Quality Improvement Direction

    A. Vision of organization

        1. What is the vision of the organization?

        2. Is the vision supported by the organization?

    B. Mission of organization

        1. Is the mission of the organization customer-focused?

        2. Does everyone know what the mission is?

        3. Do all teams have similar missions?

    C. Purpose of organization

        1. What are the long-term goals of the organization toward improvement of quality and reducing defects?

        2. Is there a long-range system plan for quality?

        3. What quality initiatives are being implemented?

    D. Continuous improvement

        1. How is the organization achieving continuous improvement?

        2. Give examples of improvement.

        3. What are the vital few problems being studied?

        4. Is there evidence that QPC tools and the TAPS model are being used by teams?

    E. Organizational chart of Quality Control System

        1. Describe the management team composition.

        2. How are breakthrough teams chartered?

        3. How are TAPS teams organized?

II. Quality Leadership

    A. How have quality correlates been implemented in the system?

        1. Work on the System

        2. Adopt Lead Management Principles

        3. Workers Assess Own Quality

        4. Continuous Improvement of Quality

    B. How is management focusing on and supporting quality?

    C. What barriers have been eliminated?

    D. What domain of organizational health is the campus/department focusing on for improvement?

        1. Is there an action plan for improvement?

        2. Is it being implemented?

    E. What control charts (check sheets) is management using to check administrative processes?

    F. What control charts is management using to check other processes or outputs?

    G. How many TAPS teams are operating?

        1. How successful have they been?

        2. How does management support the teams?

III. Customer Input

    A. Outline the processes for determining customers' expected outcomes, and assessment of current quality of product.

    B. Customer feedback: List some customer groups who have given satisfactory or "bragging" feedback.

CUSTOMER	POSITIVE FEEDBACK INDICATOR
1. _____	_____
2. _____	_____
3. _____	_____
4. _____	_____
5. _____	_____

        1. What causes customers to brag?

        2. What is the loss by not meeting the customers' needs?

        3. How does the school/department communicate with the customers?

IV. Supplier Communication

    A. What process does management have for determing quality of suppliers' products?

    B. How does management communicate your expectations with the suppliers?

V. Institution of Training

    A. What are the plans for continued training of all staff in the Quality School Correlates?

    B. How are the plans being implemented?

        1. Are estimated dates of accomplishment stated?

        2. Are methods stated as to how training will be accomplished?

        3. How will new personnel be trained?

        4. How will follow-up training be administered?

    C. How effective is the training program? List positives and negatives.

    D. What other in-house training is occurring?

    E. What training in job skills is offered?

VI. Site-Based and Process-Based Decision-Making

    A. Does the management team have full responsibility for system planning?

    B. Is there trust between the principal/director and the management team?

    C. Is the management team using a quality assurance plan to collect useful data?

    D. Is the data used to focus on customer quality opportunities?

    E. Are teams being chartered for solving the vital few problems?

    F. Is authority given to TAPS teams to solve process based problems?

SEVEN OBSTACLES TO AVOID

OBSTACLE 1: BOSS MANAGEMENT

Boss management will ruin all efforts toward quality improvement. Trust is the cornerstone of CIM; boss management topples the Tower of Trust. If boss management prevails at the top, the quality initiatives will never take on a life of their own. They will be treated as programs to implement by mandate, and mandating change from the top works only when those below are empowered by the change. If true empowerment does not occur, then the change will be given only lip service, and the status quo will continue. If mid-managers are mostly boss managers, they will implement the changes reluctantly, always protecting their turf. They will never release enough control of the processes to allow employee self-assessment and continuous improvement to work. Most problems associated with the implementation of CIM come from mid-level boss managers. Lower-level managers, such as department heads, team leaders, and teachers can trap power at their level and prevent empowerment of others—especially the students. Unless students are empowered to be responsible for their own learning, then quality learning will not exist.

What does an organization do with boss managers? The initial approach should be training, but if training does not help, an outside consultant can be called in to work with the manager. If no noticeable change soon is apparent, then the manager must be moved, or the position structured so that the boss manager does not possess significant power. Give the power to the management team or to self-directed teams.

OBSTACLE 2: NO TIME

CIM requires time for planning, teaming, training, and communicating. If managers cannot prioritize their time to deal with day-to-day activities and preventive measures, then firefighting will continue to be the usual method of conducting business. Teams need to use the tools to save time, since the tools allow for processing information without excessive discussion. Teams should be able to conduct their business in one hour. (Committees take several hours because QPC tools are not used.)

Time will be saved by focusing on the vital few problems rather than the trivial many. When other problems surface, management should guard against adding them to the list. If a problem is urgent, then it should be substituted for one of the vital few, especially if time is a factor. The astute manager will recognize when people are stressed because of time limits. He or she will pull back projects and allow time for completion. This is a good time to celebrate the success obtained up to that point.

OBSTACLE 3: STIMULUS–RESPONSE LEGISLATURES AND STATE EDUCATION AGENCIES

Legislatures operate on a short-term basis: There is no mechanism for long-range planning. Legislators must accomplish something during their term of office, so they look for quick fixes. They are pressed by the press and taxpayers to hold school districts accountable. They choose to do this by state testing and accreditation audits. Accountability to legislators and state education agency decision-makers means checking for short-term gains. Rewards and punishments are given for end-of-year performance scores. In order to comply with this stimulus–response system of blaming the schools and workers for the problems, school districts must adopt quick-fix, costly programs. When school districts can, they manipulate the numbers and play games with the information given to the state. The legislature reacts with additional mandates requiring more close supervision of schools, tougher and newer tests, and competition among schools (recognizing the winners and punishing the losers). The system promoted by most legislators and state education officials is the costly system of rework and recycle that will never produce the quality they really want. This insane system is counterproductive for schools wanting to pursue long-term planning and continuous improvement of processes through worker empowerment. Most schools will succumb to the pressures from above, and will not take on the long-term commitment to change how they manage processes. The loss will be the state policymakers' as they try one reform after another, to no avail.

OBSTACLE 4: THE REWARD FOR STATUS QUO

Change in a political environment is difficult to accomplish. The very nature and purpose of politics is to ensure the status quo. Change cause discontent, angry special-interest groups, and unhappy constituents. Unless the superintendent can get a long-term commitment from the school board for the change to CIM, it will probably be doomed. There will be those in the community who will oppose any change from the status quo. Workers and managers who have power in the old system will attempt to derail any changes that dilute their control. They will apply pressure to school boards through letters and at board meetings. Many times it is the superintendent who loses his/her job. Little wonder that superintendents who are "change agents" have an average tenure of less than four years: The new superintendent comes in and scraps all the work done by his/her predecessor. One reason the Japanese are able to maintain quality initiatives is the long-term tenure of their CEOs. In America,

CEOs change companies frequently and often lose their positions if (for example) quarterly earnings are not what the board of directors has desired. The reward is for the short-term planners, and little change. Time will tell if the present governance system for schools will be able to foster the drastic changes needed for schools to become quality schools.

OBSTACLE 5: NO COMMITMENT BY TOP MANAGEMENT

If the superintendent of the school district is not committed to CIM, then the district will not adopt CIM. If the principal is not committed, then the school will not adopt CIM. If the classroom teacher is not committed to CIM, then the students will not adopt quality improvement practices. Millions of dollars are spent on education, with less-than-satisfactory results. It is not that schools have not improved since the 1950s. They have in fact improved dramatically. However, the expectations of schools since the 1980s have increased even more dramatically. The need for educated workers to improve the processes they own has caused this increase in expectations. To make the changes needed requires schools to adopt the same principles of CIM that companies needing these educated workers have. The solution is simple: Hire the best superintendent or principal that money can buy, who is a change agent with a committed vision to excellence. Then get out of his/her way and support the change. This has proven successful even in many isolated cases in various parts of the nation. The problem is that the salaries pale in comparison to salaries given to company CEOs. The talented superintendent or principal does not stay long. He or she goes into consultant work, private business, or college-level teaching. Look at the résumés of talented people in these fields and you will often find they were school principals for only a short time before moving on with their careers. These positions must stop becoming steppingstones to other careers for those with the talent to stay on and help make the change from ordinary to quality schools.

OBSTACLE 6: GRADES AND THE BELL-SHAPED CURVE

As long as grades are the prime motivator for learning, students either will do only enough to make the grade they want, or will not work for grades at all. Grades are a stimulus–response system of attempting to motivate students with reward and punishment. Any secondary school teacher will confess that grades are poor motivators. If grades worked, then students who make C or below would strive to make better grades. Experience shows this is not true. Students who fail, or make D's or C's, continue to make the same grades because these reinforce their belief that they cannot do the work needed for the higher grades. The system of bell-shape grade distributions means that grades are competitive.

Only the top 10 percent make the A's, and the next 20 percent make the B's, and so forth. Teachers who give more A's and B's than this are accused of being too easy—of grade inflation and lowering standards. Grading is perceived by students as what teachers do to them. Ask the average student what his or her grade in a certain class was and he/she will say "The teacher gave me a C," not "I made a C." Some schools may even be able to get rid of grades as a way of measuring learning. Most will not have this choice, though, because those few who achieve in school by making the grades will lobby for the continuation of this method, since it rewards them. The best that schools can do in these circumstances is reduce the reliance on grades as a motivator. Learning for power should be the motivator! Useful learning will give students the power to make something out of their lives. Bell-shaped curves as appropriate grade distributions should be abolished. The recognition should go to the teachers, who can make learning easy and who are able to create success for all students.

OBSTACLE 7: FOCUSING ON ABILITY INSTEAD OF EFFORT

While the Japanese public school system leaves much to be desired as a model for U.S. schools, the Japanese are worth emulating in some areas—such as the cooperative environment instilled in the elementary grades. The other is their recognition for effort rather than ability. All students are considered to have the same ability, so the schools concentrate on inducing effort. Recognition is given for both cooperative efforts and individual efforts. There are no ability tests or IQ tests, and students are not grouped by ability or tracked. (Of course, this is not the case in competitive Japanese secondary schools, where the national tests separate the students who will go to college from those who will not.)

American schools are intent on rewarding ability; every student's performance is measured throughout his or her school career. Norm-referenced tests determine whether the student is in a low group for reading, in gifted and talented, in an at-risk program, or just average. Colleges accept only those students who can score high on the SAT or ACT tests. For those students who are not test-takers or who have given up because some test indicated they were below average in ability, there is only one alternative—dropping out physically or mentally from school. Think of the billion-dollar-per-year waste that dropouts cause to be lost from American productivity at a time when we are chasing the Japanese and other Asian economies. How many of these students could become great leaders, scientists, or business people will not be known until ability tests and norm-referenced tests are abolished. When effort is praised, all students will be able to compete equally. When cooperative effort is praised, all students benefit, and the groundwork is laid for the future worker in the CIM companies of the twentieth century.

Deming's Fourteen Points as a Classroom Model for Quality

A manager is defined as anyone who manages others.
This includes teachers, who manage students.

Point 1: Create Constancy of Purpose for the Improvement of Student Learning and Service

No classroom will be successful unless students understand the purpose of the learning offered therein. The teacher should spend the first week of school (or longer) helping students to understand why the subject at hand is important. Unless it has meaning, most students will not do quality work on it. Involving the students in developing a mission statement for the class is one way to increase relevancy. Using a cause-and-effect diagram to brainstorm which classroom practices improve learning is another. The classroom mission statement would reflect these beliefs.

Point 2: Adopt the New Philosophy

The organization's management style must be transformed from boss to lead management. Cooperation rather than competition among students, and between students and teachers, is the goal. The teacher must accept the new philosophy and teach it to the students. Teachers should ask students to define quality in their own terms. What is a quality car, wardrobe, tune? Why? What is a quality person? Who is one, and why? What is a quality assignment? Why? What is quality work? Why? Students should also be encouraged to display what they consider quality work.

Point 3: Cease Dependence on Mass Monitoring for Defects

Decrease the reliance on grades as a method of motivating students. Only a small percentage of students are truly motivated by grades (or other incentives). The majority need to see a purpose for learning, and know that caring people will support them. To decrease reliance on grades, allow students to evaluate their own work for quality. Let the students develop the criteria for evaluating the assignment. Have them place a Q on their paper when they have done quality work. Praise effort, not ability. Let the students grade an assignment and then average their grade with the teacher's grade. Allow students to grade their own homework. Let them keep track of these grades by charting their own grades. Teach control charting. Use mastery learning principles to teach mastery of what is "need to know." Don't wait for the end of the year or semester to find out that many students are making D's and F's. Monitor the learning, and correct defects early. Change what you are doing if it is not working for at least 95 percent of students. Continuous improvement means planning, doing the planned thing on a small scale, checking the results, and then implementing the full plan for all students if it is more-or-less sure to be successful.

Point 4: Reduce Variation in the Input from the Suppliers

Parents are the main suppliers to the classroom. Develop two-way communication with parents on a weekly basis. Develop a partnership agreement with all your parents, possibly even in the form of a working agreement . One school's contract between parents and teachers is found on the next page.

Point 5: Improve Constantly and Permanently the System of Student Learning and Service

Responsibility for transforming the system rests with the classroom manager. Total Quality Management does not allow for blaming the worker, customer, or supplier for defects. It requires input from the customer and acting on that information to improve. Managers act on the system, workers work in the system. Managers act on the system by continuous use of Plan-Do-Check-Act, using the TAPS Model. The classroom manager must have the authority to make the necessary changes.

Point 6: Institute Training and Retraining

Everyone in the system must understand lead management principles, control theory and reality therapy, the Team Approach to Problem Solving model, and the Quality Process Control tools—such as brainstorming, fishbone, consensus methods, flow diagraming, and Pareto diagraming. All persons must be able, with practice, to use SPC tools such as histograms, control charts, and run charts. Students also should learn these concepts.

PARENT/TEACHER WORKING AGREEMENT

Dear Parent,

    Educating your child takes the combined efforts of the school staff, your child, and you. I wish to make this a productive year for your child by coming to agreement with you on what is best for him/her. To do this, we must keep in mind that you are my supplier and I am your customer. You supply me with your child every day. As my supplier, I expect you to ensure that:

A. Your child will:

1. Be in school on time, every day, unless illness prevents attendance.
2. Have a good night's sleep.
3. Eat a good breakfast before classes begin.
4. Set aside time for homework each night.
5. Arrive at school with all books and materials.
6. Follow the rules of the school.
7. Reduce the amount of TV viewing, and set aside daily time for reading.

B. You will:

1. Inform me when your child is unhappy about school or this class.
2. Attend parent conferences at a mutually convenient time.
3. Inform me when you have concerns about the child or the class.
4. Reinforce the class emphasis on problem-solving by carrying out this plan at home with your child.
5. Help your child set goals and plans to reach those goals.

    On the other end, you are my customer and I am your supplier, since I am providing your child with the necessary tools to become educated. As my customer your satisfaction is very important to me. Therefore, I agree to:

1. Keep a folder of your child's continuous improvement projects that can be reviewed by you and your child at any time.
2. Teach your child how to track his/her own progress and assess his/her own work for quality.
3. Evaluate your child on the basis of mastery of quality work, resulting from continuous improvement projects, thereby allowing him/her to have pride in workmanship.
4. Eliminate fear from the classroom, thereby enhancing your child's self-esteem.
5. Provide a wide variety of instructional approaches to allow your child to succeed, no matter his/her learning style.
6. Provide classroom assignments and projects that are exciting, meaningful, and purposeful, thereby enhancing your child's enthusiasm for learning.
7. Teach and provide opportunities for your child to work cooperatively in groups on team projects.
8. Teach your child to assume responsibility for his/her own education by providing him/her with the necessary tools for learning.
9. Teach and provide opportunities for your child to learn the importance of helping all classmates to succeed.
10. Teach your child problem-solving techniques and allow him/her to practice this whenever personal or group problems occur.
11. Teach your child how to appraise his/her own work, and that of classmates for the purpose of continuous improvement.

Signature (parent) _____ Date _____

Signature (teacher)_____ Date _____

Point 7: Institute Leadership

Classroom managers must put into practice the principles of lead management. These managers are responsible for the following to improve quality:

1. Discover and remove barriers that prevent students from taking pride in their work.

2. Know and be able to model quality work by, for example, demonstrating quality assignments, and allowing students to develop criteria for quality assignments.

3. Teach at the student's level of understanding.

4. Involve students in planning for how the content will be taught.

Point 8: Drive Out Fear

Teachers should not use criticism, fear, or coercion to attempt to get students to perform their work. It is the teacher's responsibility to maintain or improve the organizational health of the classroom; change and quality cannot take place in a classroom that has this type of poor health. Students must have faith that the class satisfies their needs for belonging, recognition, fun, and choices. The classroom manager's knowledge and use of control theory and reality therapy techniques will help achieve these results. The single most fear-producing system used in schools is grades. Reduce the reliance on grades for motivating students. Successful learning occurs when the activities are fun and intrinsically rewarding. Use constructive feedback rather than criticism. Give a student positive feedback four times for every time you must talk with him/her about a problem.

Criticism	Constructive Feedback
concerns the past	concerns present/future
opinion, judgment	facts
use of you	use of we
negative	positive
not timely	timely
focus on person	focus on behavior
blaming	training

Point 9: Break Down Barriers Between Work Groups

Teachers should share their classroom successes and failures with other teachers. Teachers should work in teams that focus on the students rather than on the subject matter. TAPS teams of teachers should be formed to discuss, assess, and plan for quality. Students should be organized into learning teams, to break down barriers among them.

Point 10: Eliminate Slogans, Exhortations, and Goals for the Work Force

Slogans, exhortations, and goals without plans are a waste of time and energy. All teachers should have a plan for what will be taught and how. Students should be involved in the planning whenever possible. Teachers should work with students at the beginning of the year to set goals for each six weeks, each semester, and the full school year. Goals should be reassessed periodically.

Point 11: Eliminate Numerical Quotas; Substitute Leadership

Deming believes that quotas and numerical goals impede quality more than do any other working conditions. Grades based solely on paper-and-pencil tests discourage students from taking an active role in learning and promote isolationism because of competition.

Point 12: Remove Barriers to Pride of Workmanship

Trust is vital to the Total Quality classroom. Without trust (and other empowerments, such as teaming and problem-solving), students will lack encouragement to achieve quality work. Only classrooms that operate with a clearly defined mission statement, allowing students to set high goals with meaningful assignments, will produce active, enthusiastic, lifelong learners. Every effort must be made to eliminate busy work, traditional grading scales, dependence on worksheets, and boredom. Pride in workmanship comes from working to resolve real problems, often within a team setting.

Point 13: Institute a Vigorous Program of Education and Retraining

Teacher training is the key to quality in the classroom. Training should include teaching strategies, Total Quality Approach principles, classroom management through lead management principles, and teaming skills. Training should be based on the needs of teachers. There should be some follow-up to all training through use of coaches and mentors.

Point 14: Take Action to Accomplish the Transformation

Team-based decision-making will assist teachers in advancing Deming's points. Statistical information must be available for teachers to study. All staff members should acquire a precise idea of how to improve quality continuously. The initiative must come from management. The Shewhart Cycle of "Plan, Do, Check/Study, Act" should be used to accomplish quality via the following steps:

STEP 1: Study a process, to decide what change might improve it. Organize the appropriate team. Use the TAPS model. Do not proceed without a plan.

STEP 2: Carry out the tests, or make the change, preferably on a small scale.

STEP 3: Observe the effects.

STEP 4: What did we learn? Repeat the test if necessary, perhaps in a different environment. Look for side-effects.

STEP 5: Repeat Step 1, with knowledge accumulated.

STEP 6: Repeat Step 2, and onward.

BIBLIOGRAPHY

Bennis, Warren and Burt Nanus. *Leaders: The Strategies for Taking Charge.* New York: Harper & Row, 1985.

Bennis, Warren. *On Becoming a Leader.* Reading, MA: Addison-Wesley Publishing Co., Inc., 1989.

Betts, Frank. *How Systems Thinking Applies to Education.* Educational Leadership, November, 1992.

Blanchard, Kenneth and Paul Hersey. *Management of Organizational Behavior: Utilizing Human Resources.* Englewood Cliffs, NJ: Prentice-Hall, Inc., 1982.

Bonstingl, John Jay. *Schools of Quality.* Alexandria, VA: Association for Supervisors and Curriculum Development Publications, 1992.

Borgers, William E. *A Return To Discipline.* Houston: Unpublished manuscript, 1979.

Byham, William C. *Zapp! The Lightning of Empowerment.* New York: Harmony Books, 1990.

Byham, William C., Richard S. Wellins and Jeanne M. Wilson. *Empowered Teams.* San Francisco/Oxford: Jossey-Bass Publishers, 1991.

Byrnes, Margaret A., Robert A. Cornesky and Lawrence Byrnes. *The Quality Teacher: Implementing Total Quality Management In The Classroom.* Bunnell, FL: Cornesky and Associates Press, 1992.

Carlzon, Jan. *Moments of Truth.* Cambridge, MA: Ballinger Publishing Co., 1987.

Covey, Stephen R. *Principle-Centered Leadership.* Provo, UT: The Institute for Principle-Centered Leadership, 1990.

Covey, Stephen R. *The Seven Habits of Highly Effective People.* New York: Simon and Schuster, Inc., 1989.

Deal, Terrence E. and Allen A. Kennedy. *Corporate Cultures.* New York: Addison-Wesley Publishing Co., Inc., 1982.

Debono, Edward. *The Six Thinking Hats.* Boston: Little, Brown and Company, 1985.

Deming, W. Edwards. *Out of the Crisis.* Cambridge, MA: Productivity Press or Washington, D.C.: The George Washington University, MIT-CAES, 1982.

Drucker, Peter F. *Managing the Non-Profit Organization.* New York: Harper Collins, 1990.

Fairman, Marvin. *Organizational Health Manual.* Fayetteville, AR: Organizational Health: Diagnostic and Development Corporation, 1979.

Garfield, Charles. *Peak Performers: The Heroes of American Business.* New York: Avon Books, 1986.

Glasser, William. *Control Theory in the Classroom.* New York: Harper & Row, 1986.

Glasser, William. *Schools Without Failure.* New York: Harper & Row, 1975.

Glasser, William. *The Identity Society.* New York: Harper & Row, 1975.

Glasser, William. *The Quality School.* New York: Harper & Row, 1990.

Glasser, William. *The Quality School Curriculum.* Phi Delta Kappan, May, 1992.

Glasser, William. *The Quality School Teacher.* New York: Harper & Row, 1993.

Goldratt, Elihu M. and Jeff Cox. *The Goal.* Croton-on-Hudson, NY: North River Press, 1992.

Hersey, Paul. *The Situational Leader.* New York: Warner, 1984.

Hunter, Madeline. *Improved Instruction.* El Segundo, CA: Tip Publications, 1976.

Ishikawa, K. *What Is Total Quality Control? The Japanese Way.* Englewood Cliffs, NJ: Prentice Hall, 1985.

Johnson, David W. and Roger T. Johnson, Edythe Johnson Holubec. *Circles of Learning: Cooperation in the Classroom.* Edina, MN: Interaction Book Co., 1986.

Juran, J.M. *Juran On Planning For Quality.* Cambridge, MA: Productivity Press, 1988.

Langford, David P. *Total Quality Learning*. Training seminar, June 1993.

Leonard, James F. *How to Use Data in the Total Quality School*. Quality Network News, November, 1991.

Patterson, Jerry L. *Leadership for Tomorrow's Schools*. Alexandria, VA: Association for Supervisors and Curriculum Development Publications, 1993.

Peters, Tom and Robert H. Waterman, Jr. *In Search of Excellence*. New York: Harper & Row, 1982.

Peters, Tom J. and Nancy Austin. *A Passion for Excellence: The Leadership Difference*. New York: Random House, 1985.

Peters, Tom J. *Thriving on Chaos*. New York: Harper & Row, 1987.

Savary, Louis M. *Creating Quality Schools*. Arlington, VA: American Association of School Administrators, 1992.

Scherkenbach, W. W. *The Deming Route to Quality and Productivity*. Rockville, MD: Mercury Press/ Fairchild Publications, 1987.

Schmoker, Mike and Richard B. Wilson. *Transforming Schools Through Total Quality Education*. Phi Delta Kappan, January, 1993.

Scholtes, P. R. *The Team Handbook*. Madison, WI: Joiner Associates, 1988.

Scholtes, Peter R. *An Elaboration on Deming's Teachings on Performance Appraisal*. Madison,WI: Joiner Associates, 1987.

The National Center to Save Our Schools. *Applying TQM*. Total Quality and Site-Based Management Journal, January/ February,1993.

Tribus, Myron. *Deployment Flow Charting*. Los Angeles: Quality and Productivity, Inc., 1989.

Tribus, Myron. *The Application of Quality Management Principles in Education, at Mt. Edgecumbe High School, Sitka, Alaska*. November, Unpublished manuscript, 1990.

Walton, Mary. *The Deming Management Method*. New York: Perigee/Putnam, 1986.

Zemke, Ron with Dave Walonick. *Constructing Surveys to Collect Customer Data: The Non-Statistician's Approach*. Total Quality and Site-Based Management Journal, March/April, 1993.